A Son of Kelso on the Somme

From the Somme to Passchendaele
...... and back across the Western Front

One man's journey through life in
Frontline Trenches during World War One.

**Charlie Robeson (Military Medal),
225th Field Company, Royal Engineers**

Includes experiences of life on the
Home Front for his fiancée Winifred Scott.

Dr Derek Robeson

The
**Meltwater
Press Kelso**

First published in 2014 by

The
**Meltwater
Press Kelso**

7 Broomlands Gardens, Kelso, Roxburghshire, TD5 7SS

Text copyright, unless stated, Dr Derek Robeson 2014

Photographic copyright is acknowledged in captions

ISBN: 978-0-9929698-0-6

British Library Cataloguing-in-Publication Data

A catalogue record of this book is available on request

Book designed, printed and bound in the Scottish Borders by Footeprint, Jedburgh, Scotland

All proceeds from the sale of this book go to
Poppyscotland & Help for Heroes

Contents

FOR FREEDOM

Dedicated to

Charlie Robeson & his wife Winnie & their children
Robin, Margaret, James & Mabel

In memory of

Soldiers of the Royal Engineers Field Companies in World War One

&

243 men of Kelso and District who fell in the Great War for Civilisation 1914 – 1918

The battles in which Charlie Robeson fought on the Western Front

*This photograph was taken after fierce fighting,
in the German Spring Offensive, of March 1918.*

1916 – The Battles of the Somme, France

The Battle of Thiepval Ridge

The Battle of the Ancre

Capture of the Schwaben Redoubt and Stuff Trench near Beaumont Hamel

The Last Battle of the Somme

1917 – The Third Battles of Ypres, Belgium

The Battle of Pilckem Ridge

The Battle of Langemarck

The Battle of Menin Road Ridge

The Battle of Polygon Wood

The Second Battle of Passchendaele

1918 – The First Battles of the Somme, France

Operation Michael – The German Spring Offensive – The Battle of St. Quentin

The Actions at the Somme Crossings

The Battle of Bapaume

The Battle of Rosieres

(Brief descriptions of the battles are given in this book)

Foreword

The Great War was one of the defining moments of European and indeed World History. As a result of the war, big changes were made to the map of Europe; great Empires ceased to exist and new nations became powerful; the style of government in most countries changed considerably; the social structure of European society was transformed and the way of life was greatly altered from pre-war years.

When we study this great conflict, it is usual to consider the actions of the Great Powers as they interacted with, and opposed, each other, to discuss the military and naval tactics, technological advances, set piece battles and great turning points. Noted military historians still debate the decisions and tactics of the politicians and generals – we still can't even agree what exactly caused the war and who was responsible!

What we often forget in the midst of this, is the impact that the war had on the people who lived through it and the lasting effect that it had on those who survived it. It is not always correct to call them the lucky ones.

The beauty of this book, is that it makes this point so clearly. Explaining, as it does, the strategic decisions and actions of the Great Powers, then looking at how these impacted on one Army, one Division, one Company of soldiers and how this in turn, influenced the life of one soldier and his family, provides an eloquent testimony of the experience of war, at that time.

Derek Robeson, here recording the war experience of his grandfather and grandmother, is not only collating the story for his family but is also paying a moving tribute to all the men and women who were involved in this terrible conflict. They were normal human beings, not super beings, with all the usual interests and talents – rugby, cricket, golf, reading, dancing and so on. Yet, their experiences during the war were far from normal. It is all too typical of the men and women who lived through the war, that Charlie Robeson chose not to speak much of his experiences. However, he clearly never forgot them and the letters, photographs, postcards and documents that Charlie and his wife Winnie kept, provide a clear and first hand account of a time of great challenge. They are a priceless record of family history.

We are lucky indeed, that Derek has chosen to share them with us.

Charlie Robertson
Rector (retired), Kelso High School.
Eckford
June, 2014

Introduction

This book was compiled with respect to my grandparents, whose letters and photographs we rediscovered after my parent's death. Charlie Robeson rarely spoke of his time in the war but my family believes that the story contained in his letters home to his fiancée Winnie, (my grandmother) and the material and photographs they gathered are worth sharing. This is the true story, like so many others at the time, of an ordinary man and woman, caught up in extraordinary events.

Purpose of the book, layout and material acknowledgements

The aim of the book is to share the personal letters, photographs and experiences of one Kelso man and his fiancée, during the worst conflict the world has ever known. It follows the life of a young Borderer who survived two years in Frontline trenches on the battlefields of the Western Front. At the same time, it highlights what his fiancée was experiencing, as a nurse, on the Home Front. To make it more meaningful, information is included about family life in the Borders before and after the war. Charlie Robeson lived in Kelso prior to 1914 and returned to Kelso in 1919 to marry Winnie. Together, they lived a full and happy family life.

As regards writing about the facts of the war, rather than rewriting the already well documented history, short summaries of actual events are recorded at appropriate points. These are largely written in the words of referenced sources and are acknowledged alongside. All the battles described in this book are the actual battles in which Charlie Robeson fought. Much of the historical detail included herein has been extracted from two highly informative websites; 'The Long Long Trail' by Chris Baker and 'BBC History.' Chris McCarthy's books 'The Somme' and 'Passchendaele' were invaluable. The official War Diary of the 225th Field Company, Royal Engineers (Charlie Robeson's Company), is used throughout the book as a timeline. The War Diary lists where the Company was, what the men were doing and what happened on a day-to-day basis. The surviving War Diaries are available from the National Archives in London. Crown copyright has expired for the War Diaries and copyright on most official war photographs has similarly expired. Many of the war photographs used are reproduced from the Haig Papers, part of the National Library of Scotland collection. Permission to reproduce material from these sources is kindly acknowledged. Some images are from the Imperial War Museum. Much of the remaining material comes from the author's family collection. Every effort was made to trace other photographic copyright, though some gaps remain. Sources of information are provided throughout the text. The use of all this material is duly and gratefully acknowledged.

A primary objective of the book was to have the family photographs and letters reproduced before they faded from view and to piece them together, in a meaningful way, as a family record. It serves also as a record of the activities of the 225th Field Company Royal Engineers during the Great War. This book is also an educational resource, intended for upper secondary school-age children but hopefully, it will have a wider appeal, to all age groups, as an interesting piece of social history.

Timeline for Charlie Robeson's experiences in the battles of the Great War on the Western Front

Throughout 1914 and 1915 Charlie Robeson played professional Rugby League (under contract) for Oldham RLFC. Charlie wanted to enlist when war began but due to professional rugby team commitments, was unable to. In February 1916 he joined Kitchener's Army.

1914

28th June	Archduke Franz Ferdinand assassinated.
1st – 4th August	Main countries declare war on each other.
4th August	Germany invades Belgium. Britain declares war on Germany.
Mid August	British Expeditionary Force (BEF) deploys on Franco-Belgian border.
23rd August	Japan declares war on Germany. Battle of Mons and start of retreat to the Marne.
6th September	Allied counter attack at the Marne. German retreat begins.
19th October	First Battle of Ypres begins.

1915

22nd April	Second Battle of Ypres begins.
25th April	Start of Gallipoli Campaign with Turkey.
7th May	RMS Lusitania sunk by German submarine.
23rd September	The Battle of Loos.
19th December	British Commander, Sir John French dismissed. Sir Douglas Haig becomes Commander-in-Chief of the British Army.

1916

21st February	The Battle of Verdun (between the French and Germans) begins.
24th February	Sapper Charlie Robeson (Regimental No. 164754) enlists with the British Army as a volunteer Royal Engineer. Training begins.
24th April	Charlie mobilised to fight in France.
31st May	Battle of Jutland, the only major sea battle of the war.
1st July	Assault phase of Battle of the Somme begins. 60,000 casualties on first day.
29th July	Charlie crosses the English Channel to France. He disembarks at Le Havre and sails up the River Seine to the main British military camp at Rouen and travels inland to fight in the Battle of the Somme.
27th August	Von Falkenhayn dismissed. Hindenburg and Ludendorff take over command of the German Army.
15th September	Tanks appear on Somme battlefield for first time at Flers-Courcelette.
26th – 28th September	Charlie takes part in the Battle of Thiepval Ridge.
1st October – 11th November	Charlie takes part in the Battle of Ancre Heights, including Stuff Trench and the final successful attack and capture of the Schwaben Redoubt near Beaumont Hamel. This engagement marks the final conflict in the Battle of the Somme, during 1916.
Mid November	Battle of Verdun closes. Both sides exhausted.
18th November	Battle of the Somme officially closes.
1st December	Charlie is moved to Ypres (Canal Bank) on Flanders Fields in Belgium, in preparation for a new offensive against the Germans during 1917.
6th December	Asquith government falls. Lloyd George becomes Prime Minister.

1917

12th March	First Russian Revolution begins.
17th March	Germany withdraws the Western Front to the Hindenburg Line.
6th April	America declares war on Germany.
9th April	Battle of Arras. Vimy Ridge captured.
16th April	First French Army mutinies after disaster on Chemin des Dames.
7th June	Battle of Messines begins with detonation of 19 massive mines.
31st July	Third Battle of Ypres begins. Summer rain starts.
31st July – 2nd August	Charlie fights in the Battle of Pilckem Ridge.
16th – 18th August	Charlie fights in the Battle of Langemarck.
20th – 25th September	Charlie fights in the Batttle of Menin Road Ridge.
26th September	Charlie fights in the Battle of Polygon Wood.
4th October	Second Battle of Passchendaele, part of Third Ypres campaign.
26th October – 10th November	Charlie fights in the Second Battle of Passchendaele.
10th November	Third Battle of Ypres ends.
17th November	Armistice between Russia and Germany.
20th November	The Battle of Cambrai begins. The first massed tank battle.

1918

26th January	Charlie Robeson's Division is moved back to The Somme.
21st March	Final German (Spring) Offensive (Operation Michael) begins on the Somme. Charlie is based directly opposite the Germans' main point of attack, on the Hindenburg Line at St. Quentin.
21st – 23rd March	Charlie takes part in the Battle of St. Quentin.
24th – 26th March	Charlie takes part in Actions at the Somme Crossings.
26th March	General Foch takes overall control of allied armies in France.
26th – 27th March	Charlie fights in Battle of Rosieres.
30th March	Charlie Robeson wins the Military Medal for Bravery in the Field. Due to devastatingly heavy casualties, Charlie and what is left of the 39th Division, are withdrawn from the Front Line.
4th April	After 2 years on the Front Line, Charlie Robeson's Division is moved nearer to Calais to protect the Channel Ports and to train incoming US troops.
9th April	Second German attack, Ypres Salient.
27th April	Third German attack, Chemin des Dames.
1st July	Fourth German attack at the Marne.
2nd November	The last allied assault begins.
9th November	The Kaiser abdicates.
11th November	BEF arrives in Mons, exactly where they had started in 1914. German Armistice signed in a railway carriage in the Forest of Compiegne.

1919

2nd March	Charlie Robeson is transferred to Army Reserve for demobilisation and return home.
28th June	Treaty of Versailles signed, officially ending the war.

(Source – The Great War Explained)

Overview of the battlefields where Charlie Robeson fought with the 39th Division, during World War I.

Jul – Dec 1916 on the Somme near Thiepval
(www.epsomandewellhistoryexplorer.org)

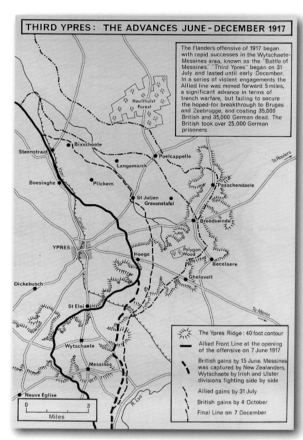

Jan – Dec 1917 at Ypres and Passchendaele
(www.gutenburg.org)

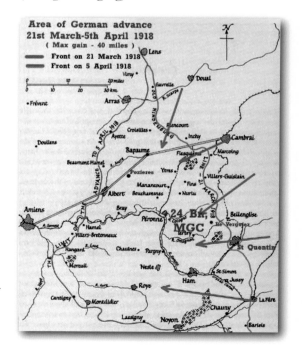

Jan – Apr 1918 back on the Somme near
St. Quentin, during the Spring Offensive
(www.kinnethmont.co.uk)

**The key battles my grandfather fought in during 1916
on the Somme and during 1917 at Passchendaele**

The key battles my grandfather fought in during 1918: The battles of the German Spring Offensive on the Somme

The Battle of St. Quentin

The Actions at the Somme Crossings

The Battle of Bapaume
All images courtesy of David Pentland, Jason Agnew and Stan Stokes, and from commemorative covers by Tony Theobald, with thanks

Summary of Charlie's life

Charles Robeson (Charlie) was born at Lilliesleaf, in the Border Country of Scotland, in November 1888. Charlie spent his youth in Lilliesleaf and moved to Kelso, to train as a saddler and harness maker when he left school. From 1907 to 1912, he played rugby for Kelso and Jedburgh, winning several Border League titles and Sevens medals. Charlie turned professional in 1913 and played Rugby League for Oldham RLFC in the 1913/14 and 1914/15 seasons. He made 44 appearances for the club, lifting the Lancashire Cup with the winning team, in the Northern Union League cup final of 1913.

In the spring of 1916, Charlie joined the Royal Engineers and between 1916 and 1918 fought with the 39th Division of the British 5th Army in France and Belgium, as part of Kitchener's Army. In the autumn of 1916, Charlie fought in the first Battle of the Somme and was involved in actions near Albert and Thiepval. His Company was present at the taking of the infamous, and near impregnable German held fortress, the Schwaben Redoubt, near Beaumont Hamel. This was the last major engagement in the Battle of the Somme. Throughout 1917 he fought the enemy, and the weather, amid the hellish mud at Passchendaele, digging frontline trenches, laying duck boards and fighting alongside the infantry. In the official War Diaries written at the time (which form the backbone of this book) there are entries for Charlie's involvement in raids on enemy trenches in the summer of 1917. It is back on the Somme, near St. Quentin, in the spring of 1918, that we get a feel for what the war in the trenches was really like, in the letters he sent home. One particularly poignant letter, started on 20th March 1918 (and finished 14 days later on 4th April), covers the period of the massively devastating German spring offensive, during which time 177,000 British soldiers became casualties. In the letter, Charlie describes being involved in bayonet charges against German machine gun posts. He survived being hit by flying bullets and two bullet holes are plain to see in one letter he sent home. Charlie won the Military Medal for *'Bravery in the Field'* during the Spring Offensive of March 1918. During this time, Charlie's Division, the 39th Division, was all but wiped out and after two years of continual fighting they were withdrawn from the Frontline. They were sent into reserve positions to train incoming American troops. After the Armistice of November 1918, Charlie had to wait until March of 1919 before he could return home to the Borders.

After the war, Charlie settled in Kelso and became a master saddler and harness maker. In 1921, he married Winifred (Winnie) Scott from Kirriemuir in Angus. In 1922, he bought over the saddlery business of W. Kerr in Roxburgh Street and traded there successfully for a number of years. In 1924 Charlie and Winnie had the first of their four children, Robert (Robin), followed by Margaret, James and Mabel. Charlie died in April 1951, at the age of only 63, hastened by the physical hardships of trench warfare and the effects of mustard and chlorine gas endured during World War I.

This book contains stories of friendship, loyalty, duty, teamwork, family commitment and family sacrifice. It is the story of a man who lived a full and happy life. For three long years between 1916 and 1919 however, it is a story of human endurance.

Charlie Robeson, Winnie Scott & other people in this story

The main person in this story is Charles Scott Hunter Robeson, known as Charlie, to his family and friends. Charlie had five sisters; Anne, Jess, Jean, Helen and Susan, and a brother James. Charlie was born in 1888 at Lilliesleaf, near Selkirk, in the Scottish Border Country. He started dating Winifred Scott before the war and corresponded with her regularly during the war. In 1908, Winnie left the family home on the Lednathie Estate in Glen Prosen, near Kirriemuir in Forfarshire, where her father was gamekeeper to the Stormonth Darlings. Along with two of her sisters, Flo and Lil, Winnie moved to Kelso to work in service in the large country houses locally. Winnie and Flo worked for the Stormonth Darlings, who also owned Eden Bank House near Stichill. Lil worked close by at Eccles House, in Berwickshire. Charlie played professional rugby league in the early war years and took up his pre-war interest as an army volunteer by joining the Royal Engineers in February 1916. He was mobilised in April and crossed over to France in July of 1916. Charlie was demobilised in March of 1919 and returned to Kelso to get married, start a family and set up in business. Major D. H. Hammonds plays a lead role in the war years, as his Company Commander and War Diary writer. Major Hammonds was killed on 30th March 1918.

Early years in Lilliesleaf & Kelso for Charlie's family

Charlie Robeson in Kelso Rugby Football strip c.1912

Charlie's grandfather in the 1830's (also called Charles)

Charlie's family home (Torwood House) in Lilliesleaf. Present are three of his five sisters: Jess, Jean and Susan (with her husband and children) and his mother, Mary Anne Hunter.

Charlie's only brother, James (2nd from left), disappeared at the age of 27 (presumed murdered) whilst taking his gold to a bank in Alaska, during the Klondyke gold rush of 1908. His sister Jess died of disease in India, after the war, at the age of 32.

Lilliesleaf village east end, as Charlie would have known it as a child c.1900.

(Authors collection)

Lilliesleaf village west end, near St. Dunstane c.1900.

(Authors collection)

Early years in Kirriemuir & Kelso for Winnie's family

Margaret Reid - Winnie's mother.

Alexander Bruce Scott – Winnie's father.

The three sisters moved to the Borders from the Forfar area, to work in country houses as house keepers, domestic servants, nannies and nurses. They communicated with each other regularly by the quickest and cheapest way, the postcard. Postcards would be sent on a daily or weekly basis to share news, to arrange meeting times and organise social events. Winnie would have visited Lilliesleaf often, once she got to know Charlie.

Charlie's fiancée, Winnie Scott (centre) with two of her four sisters, Lil (left) and Flo (right) c.1910.

Keeping in touch with postcards home to Glen Prosen & Lednathie House, Kirriemuir, Angus.

Flo writing to Lil in 1908, saying she has settled in at Eden Bank House, Stichill. Edwardian postcards depicting local scenes around Kelso were often sent between the Robeson and Scott family members (as they were by everyone at the time) as a way of keeping in touch.

Kelso Abbey. A popular local postcard sent by Winnie in 1909.

(Authors collection)

17

Postcards sent between Winnie and her sisters during 1909

Junction Pool, Kelso.

(Authors collection)

Winnie's sisters sent many postcards during 1909. This one was sent from Eden Bank House in December, from Flo, to her sisters Lil and Winnie in Edinburgh.

Postcards continued through 1910

St Johns church spire and Kelso mill buildings.

(Authors collection)

A postcard from Winnie to her sister Lil in Edinburgh during March 1910, stating that she had been to Kelso Fair and had gone to see the 'Merry Widow'.

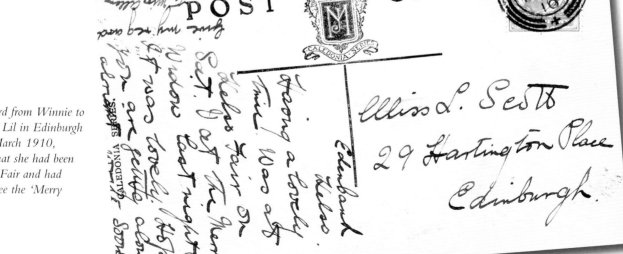

Winnie's working life

Eden Bank to the north of Kelso, where Winnie was working in 1910.

(Authors collection)

This postcard from Winnie to her sister Lil in Edinburgh in December 1910, tells Lil how much she is enjoying the dances in Kelso. Dances were held in the Corn Exchange in Wood Market. It was at one of these dances probably, that Winnie would have met Charlie. Girls would not have entered public houses in those days. Pubs were very much a male preserve.

*Winnie writing to her
sister Lil in 1910*

This postcard is written backwards, so that the postman couldn't read it. People
communicated regularly by postcard. It was the most easily accessible way.

Postcard of Lilliesleaf village just prior to WWI

(Authors collection)

Winnie visited Charlie often at his home in Lilliesleaf. There they spent much of their early months together.

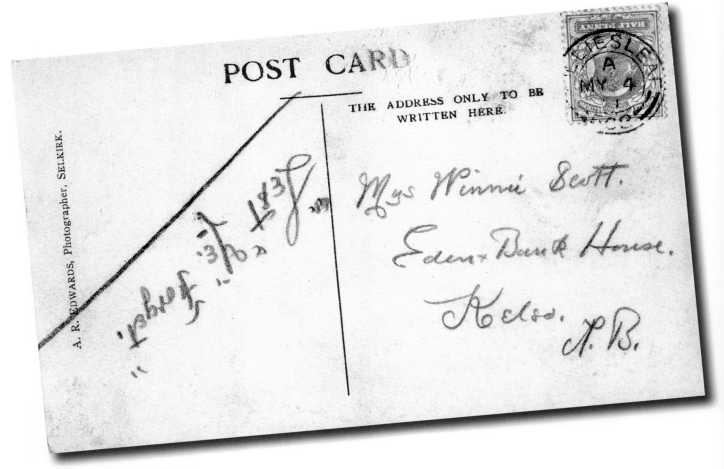

"Lest Ye Forget" Lilliesleaf.

By 1912, work and rugby commitments meant that Charlie and Winnie spent less time in Lilliesleaf and more time in Kelso. This card marked "'Lest Ye Forget" was sent by Charlie to Winnie in 1911, reminding her of the happy memories they had of the village and surrounding countryside.

Lilliesleaf was a place very dear to both their hearts, as it was where much of their courting was done. Charlie's family home lay towards the east end of the village at Torwood House. Near the west end of the village, in Hawthorn Cottage lived a well known local resident and poet, Isabella Anderson Gray. Charlie was fond of her poetry, most notably one called *'Memories'*.

Memories

I sit alone and dream of walks
Long past but pleasant still,
Of walks we've had by wood and stream
By flowery vale and hill.

Of walks along the Riddell Road,
Where trees their branches spread
A living arch of greenest leaves
That interlace o'er head

We've wandered up by Hardenburn
And to the muckle tree,
Or through the fairy-haunted glen
And ower the daisied lea.

And memory loves to linger long
By bonny Boosemill Haugh,
Where merrily the river glides
Past clumps of stately saugh.

And sweeter walks ane canna get
Than walks by fair Linthill,
Where murmuring soft the river sings
To rose and daffodil

And whiles we've daundered up the glen,
Where flowers nod by Shawburn,
And where the blossoms grow sae white
On mony an ancient thorn.

We'd cross the brig and thread the wood
And climb to Friarshaw,
Where we can see the Minto Hills
And rugged Ruberslaw.

The uplands wi' their sportive lambs,
The quiet sylvan vale,
Where birds sing in the summer morn
That flushes hill and dale.

And where around lang Lilliesleaf
With lavish hand is flung
A wreath of grace more dear to me
Than aught that ere was sung.

I sit alone and dream, and dream
Of friends that shared with me
The pleasures that have set their seal
On gracious memory.

I know not if we'll meet again
By glen and greenwood tree,
Or hear full-throated birds pour forth
Their hearts in melody;

But in that lovelier land afar,
Where all is dear and fair,
My heart shall call them unto me
And I shall meet them there.

Isabella Anderson Gray,
Hawthorn Cottage,
Lilliesleaf 1903.

Life in Kelso before the First World War

Kelso townspeople celebrate the Coronation of Edward VII in August 1902.

(Authors collection)

Kelso was a prosperous market town during the Edwardian era. It had a close-knit farming community and like other Border towns had a strong military tradition, with long established ties to the local regiment, the Kings Own Scottish Borderers (KOSB). The following postcards depict life in Kelso just prior to World War I.

Kelso Square and Town Hall c.1910.

(Authors collection)

Kelso life during the Edwardian Era
(As depicted on postcards exchanged between Charlie and Winnie)

Bridge Street c.1905. This was (and remains) the main thoroughfare to Kelso Square from the south. The Square is the centre of business and social activity.

(Authors collection)

Kelso c.1910. A view up Roxburgh Street showing daily life.

(Authors collection)

Kelso Scenes immediately before the war

Postcard of cattle being traded in Kelso Square c.1910.   (Authors collection)

Market day scenes like this, would have been familiar to Charlie & Winnie. All the street names such as; Horsemarket, Woodmarket and Coalmarket, refer to the goods that were being traded in the streets. Cattle were traded in the Square. Bulls were tethered to the bullring, still visible in the Square today.

Kelso Bridge c.1905 with cattle grazing in Bridgend Park field.   (Authors collection)

Days with Kelso Rugby Football Club

THE EDINBURGH EVENING NEWS, SATURDAY, APRIL 26, 1913.

BORDER ENTHUSIASM FOR SEVEN-A-SIDE FOOTBALL.

RANDOM

SOME IMPRESSIONS OF THIS MONTH'S SPORTS.

(BY A CITY MAN.)

England and

A tie at Melrose sports, the home of the seven-a-side game. Fairbairn, Melrose, making to drop on the ball to stem the tide of a strenuous Kelso rush. ("Evening News" Photo.)

There are some forms of sports which stand out paramount by reason of the extraordinary interest and enthusiasm which they engender in ... own with J. H. D. Watson's mixed Edinburgh seven. But the moment Watson scored, late in the second period, and the gathering realised ... all, the seven-a-side game is one of skill and judgment as well as speed and endurance. Witness, for example, how Hawick overcame at Melrose an Edinburgh University side, which on ...

A newspaper clipping from the April 1913 Melrose Sevens tournament, showing Charlie in Kelso colours (front left). 'Fairbairn (Melrose) making to drop on the ball to stem the tide of a strenuous Kelso rush'.

(Authors collection)

Kelso RFC in 1912–13 season

Back row
W Rutherford, Jas McKnight,
John McKnight, A Bulman,
J Gray, C Robeson, J Ker,
W Mair (treasurer).

Middle row
W Steel, W T Forrest, C Ogilvy
(Capt), J Melrose, W S Black,
G Fletcher.

Front Row
A Burton, J Wilson.

(Authors collection)

My grandfather's involvement with Kelso Rugby Football Club

The following is an account of the Kelso team's performance during the season 1912–13.

'The club lost their first game in the senior ranks, a friendly at Jed, 15–0. The second game was a fund raising effort against an Edinburgh XV raised by the secretary of the SRU, Mr J A Smith. Considerable improvements had been made to the Kelso ground, including new posts 35 feet high and the clubhouse at the adjoining Roxburghe bowling green was used by the teams. The visitors won easily by 21–0.

On October 12th, Kelso created the surprise of the Scottish rugby season by defeating Hawick in good weather and before a large home crowd. Kelso were first to score: a try by Steel was quickly followed by one from Rutherford, Forrest kicking the goal. The 'Black and Whites' eventually winning 11–3. The result was quickly sent to the Yetholm Shepherds Show where Sir George Douglas (of Springwood) announced the score 'amid enthusiastic cheering.'

The return, two weeks later, was given a tremendous build up and had all the ingredients of a first-class match. The North British Railway Company offered a special train and some 500 tickets were taken by the Kelso support, plus some 200 who were to travel by car.

The unchanged Kelso team were accompanied by their acknowledged mascot (Jethart Wull) who paraded the field with a black and white umbrella. In the first half, Tait scored for Hawick and Forrest kicked a goal for Kelso and the score was 3–3 at half time. Then Sutherland scored for Hawick and Burnet converted to make the final score Hawick 8– Kelso 3. Although beaten, Kelso had proved to all that they were now a force to be reckoned with.

The long-awaited Grand Bazaar was held over two days in the Corn Exchange and a magnificent £600 was realised, to put the club in a sound financial position.

In the South team to play the North at St. Andrews, no fewer than five Kelso players were listed: Spiers Black, Wattie Forrest, Johnnie Melrose, Charles Robeson and G Fletcher.

On New Years day 1913, Kelso played a XV from Glasgow raised by Mr C D Stewart. Despite the 'sixpenny' gate, there was a very large crowd to see Kelso win by 27–3.'

(Source - KRFC, A Hundred Years in Black and White)

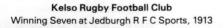

Kelso Rugby Football Club
Winning Seven at Jedburgh R F C Sports, 1913

Back Row—G Fletcher, W Steel, C Robeson, W Speirs Black.
Front Row—W T Forrest, C Ogilvy (Capt), A Bulman.

Winners of Jed Sevens 1913.

(Authors collection)

C. ROBESON
New Scottish Forward for Oldham

Oldham bound - Newspaper clipping photograph from 1913.

Professional Rugby League beckons with Oldham RLFC

Rugby League was soon to make its first in-road to the Kelso club and in June 1913 Charlie Robeson was to sign for Oldham as part of the Northern Union. Charlie was recorded in local papers as one of the 'star' performers in the Kelso pack. His place would be 'hard to fill' in the Kelso team.

The following extract appeared in a local newspaper. 'Charlie Robeson, one of the very best of Jedburgh scrummagers and described by a high authority in the game, as the best pack playing at present in Scotland, can hardly escape recognition if he keeps on improving in the way he has done this season'

Charlie turned professional in 1913 and played Rugby League for Oldham in the 1913/14 and 1914/15 seasons, turning out 44 times for the club. Competitive League games were halted in August 1915 for the duration of the war.

Charlie's first professional Rugby League pre-match photograph in Oldham team strip (back row 2nd player from right) on 6th September 1913.
They beat Dewsbury 10-8.   (ORLFC)

Charlie (centre, looking back towards camera) playing for Oldham against Huddersfield on 4th October 1913. They were beaten 19 points to 15. The player running towards the camera (in white strip) is Danny Shannon from Hawick. Danny was killed in the Great War.

A letter written by Charlie from Oldham, to Winnie back home during October 1913, after his match against Huddersfield.

7 Dundee Street.
Sunday.

My Dear 'Winnie',

I am writing you a few lines, as promised on P.C. We got back from Hud, all right, but very downhearted. We got beat 19.15 and it was all through the Referee. There were 2 Special Trains went from here, and it was the bigest gate Huddersfield have ever had. It was an awful fast game, and we led 13.3 at one time, but things seemed to alter somehow, and we just got beat. (Hard lines) We had a fine time coming home. We always have a Saloon barriage, and the singing was great. It brought me in mind of the trips with the Kelso players, only I was very quiet. They wanted me to give them one of Harry Landers, but I was not having any. I start work to-morrow morning 6.30. at a Place called Newton Heath about 4 miles from Here, so I will have to get up about 5 oclock. I dont know how I will manage it, after being used to getting up about 10. I shall have to go to bed early, and not go out at nights, so the Pictures will be a thing of the past shortly. We have got orders to be at a big Hall on Tuesdays and Thursday nights to train. It will be much nicer as the cold weather is setting in. It is very wet here to-day and I have just been and had a good bath, it helps to take the sores away. I had a letter from J. Ker again, He was asking how You were getting on, and telling me all the latest. Now Winnie I have not much more news at present, but will write sometime through the week, and tell You how I get on in my new situation. Trusting this finds You well, I will stop with still the same old feeling for You.

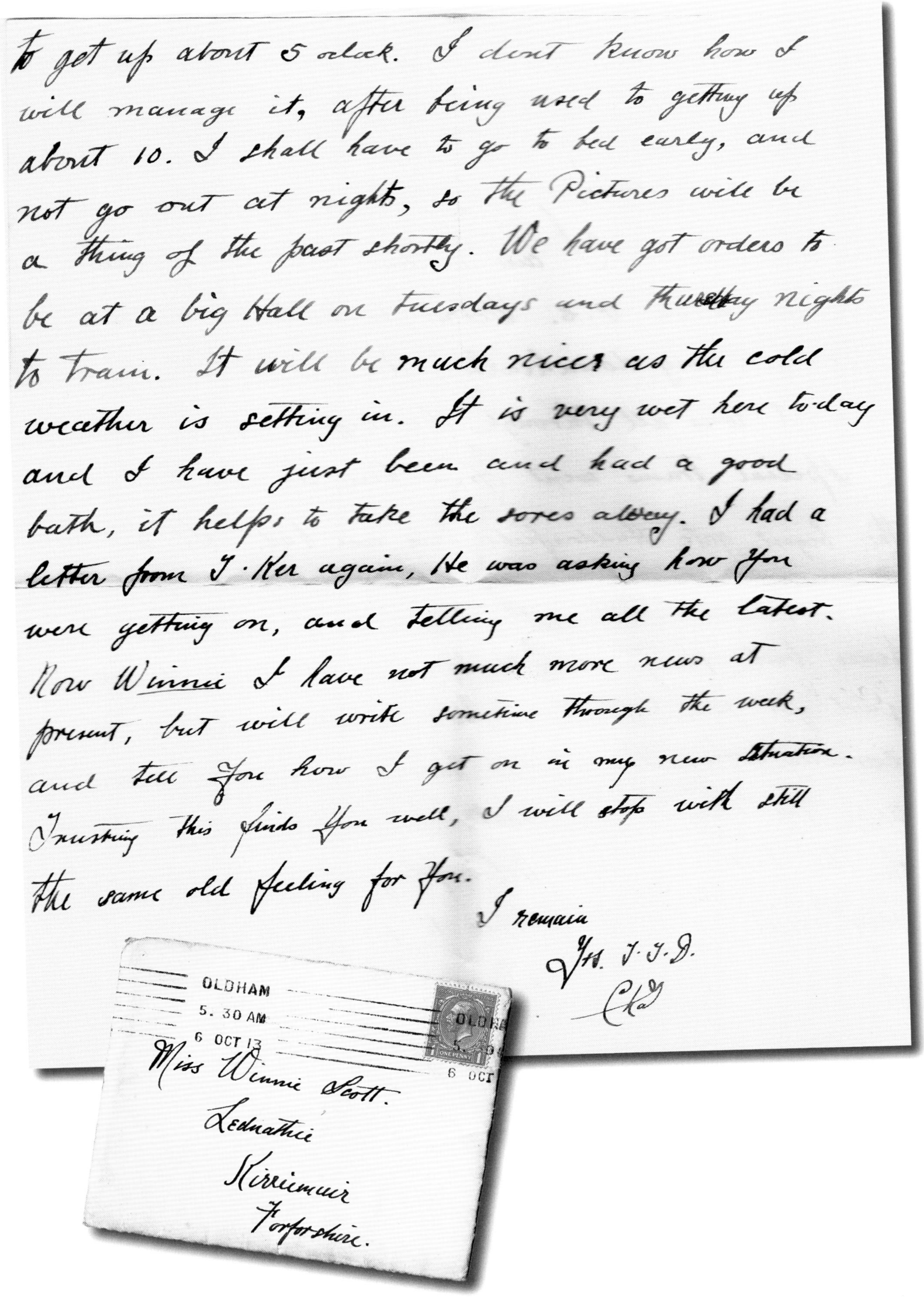

I remain
Yrs. J. I. I.
Cha

OLDHAM
5. 30 AM
6 OCT 13

ONE PENNY

Miss Winnie Scott.
Lednathie
Kirriemuir
Forfarshire.

Charlie in Oldham team colours (back row extreme right) before a league match in 1913 (ORLFC).

Charlie (in Oldham's white strip, extreme right of picture) taken with his team mates, in front of a large crowd in 1913 (ORLFC).

Oldham won the Lancashire Cup in 1913

Charlie played in the Oldham team which won the Lancashire League Cup final on Saturday 6th December 1913. 20,000 people watched Oldham beat Wigan in 'a thrilling match'. Rugby League was hugely popular amongst working men. On their return to Oldham, the local paper wrote *'thousands of people lined the streets to welcome them back and to see the cup.'*

Charlie (who was a second row forward) playing in the Lancashire Cup Final of 6th December 1913 (centre left, arms outstretched). (Authors collection)

PHOTO, HAIGH.   OLDHAM.
OLDHAM FOOTBALL CLUB SEASON 1913 - 14.
WINNERS LANCASHIRE SENIOR CUP.

Post-match Lancashire Cup winning team photograph 6th December 1913. (Charlie is standing, second row, extreme right). (ORLFC)

Postcards home to Kelso from Oldham

*22nd November 1913
- Saturday Night - Had
another win today.*

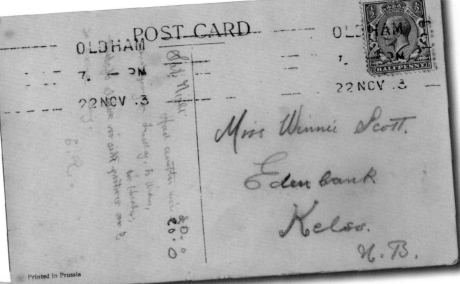

*Posted Christmas Day 1913
- We won again today…We
go to Warrington tomorrow.*

*Written backwards and dated
17th January 1914, it reads -*

Saturday Morning:

Dear Winnie,

*Got your letter this morning.
Glad you had a good time at
Eccles. We are playing at home
today. Danny Shannon is in
the team for the first time. It is
very wet here today. I will write
tomorrow.*

*With Best Love, Charlie
(C.R.).*

Oldham Remembers

It is believed that more players joined the war effort from Oldham F.C. than any other club in the Northern Union. In recognition of their efforts, a roll of honour to those who fought in the Great War was unveiled in the pavilion at Oldham club rooms on June 26th 1920 by the club President D.W. Holden. Charlie Robeson's name appears on the roll. At the head of the roll there are the seven men who are listed as 'Fallen in Action.' Danny Shannon from Hawick was the first Oldham player to be killed in action, whilst serving with the 7th Cameron Highlanders in September 1915. Another Borders club player who turned professional and went to Oldham was Billy Jardine from Jedburgh. Billy was invalided out of the army and died in 1916. He had played in 164 games, scored 26 tries and dropped 60 goals. *(From information kindly supplied by Michael Turner, ORLFC).*

The 1914 -1919 roll of honour which hangs in the clubrooms at Oldham RLFC. Seven men who played professional rugby league for Oldham at the beginning of the war, died during the war (Fallen in Action). (ORLFC)

Participation in other Local Sports before the war

Charlie was a very fit man and participated in many of the local Border sports and games. A newspaper extract of the time (1911) highlights this:

'Charles Robeson had a good innings at the Ancrum Games on Saturday. He was first for the wrestling and also for the running spring and second for the hop-step-leap and running high leap.'

Professional Wrestling Match at Morebattle Games

Do. (12 st. and under)—1st prize, £1—
First Round.

Stood.	Fell.
W. Little, Whittingham.	J. Rutherford, Trowburn.
R. Liddle, Dundee.	T. Cousin, Hexham.
H. Dick, Newbigging.	J. Little.
S. Wallace, Southdean.	W. Roberts.
C. Robeson, Kelso.	W. Elliot, Yetholm.
G. Patterson, Swindon.	W. Tait, Yetholm.

P. Hedley, Huntford, and W. Williams, Crailing, byes.

Second Round.

W. Williams.	H. Dick.
C. Robeson.	G. Patterson.
P. Hedley.	R. Liddle.
W. Little.	S. Wallace.

Semi-Final.

C. Robeson.	W. Williams.
P. Hedley.	W. Little (3d).

Final.

P. Hedley.	C. Robeson.

A newspaper clipping of wrestling tournament results (12 stone and under category) at the Morebattle Games in 1912. Charlie gets through to the final. Prize money - £1.

Free and easy days of sports, games and peace were numbered

By the summer of 1914, war had broken out with Germany but life went on relatively normally for Charlie for the meantime. Throughout 1914 and 1915, he continued to play under contract for Oldham as a professional Rugby Football League player. Charlie had wanted to enlist at the outbreak of war but work and team commitments made that move very difficult.

Meanwhile, Charlie's fiancée Winnie had started nursing injured soldiers from the Western Front battlefields both at her home on the Lednathie Estate, Kirriemuir and in the country houses around Kelso. Winnie spent 5 years nursing hundreds of badly injured soldiers sent to the Borders to recuperate. Newton Don near Stichill became an auxiliary hospital and Eden Hall near Birgham, a military hospital.

1914 – The Beginning of a World War

A postcard of Empire troops, depicting Britain's great influence and power in 1914.   (Authors collection)

41

The build-up of men and equipment

This section lays out the prelude to war with Germany and shows how Britain (and men from the Borders) responded during the first year of a long and bitter four year campaign. The First World War would turn out to be the most horrific and bloody conflict in the history of human warfare.

Young British Soldiers were full of enthusiasm at the beginning of the war. (IWM)

Prelude to war, European context and summary of events during 1914

'Right across Europe, sovereignty and colonial issues had created great friction and left many leaders in bitter conflict in the years prior to 1914. The situation became critical in Sarajevo on the 28th of June 1914, when a Slav nationalist called Gavrilo Princip assassinated Archduke Franz Ferdinand, who was heir to the throne of the Austro-Hungarian Empire. Europe at that time was linked by a series of loose diplomatic affiliations. Britain, France and Russia had an informal working relationship. Germany, Austria-Hungary and Italy had an alliance. Within a short time, the effect of the assassination and the diplomatic complexities of the various affiliations led to war.

In early August 1914 Germany invaded neutral Belgium, to get to France. In response, Britain declared war on Germany. Germany had been viewed as a threat to Britain for some time and on the 7th August, soldiers of the British Expeditionary Force (BEF) crossed to France, to try and halt the German advance. Although the regular British Army at this time was still relatively small, swollen with enthusiastic volunteers and with French forces alongside, they were successful at the Battle of Mons in August and the Battle of the Marne in September. The battles, however, were a forerunner of worse things to come. A race to the sea quickly developed, as each side tried to gain domination over the other. The result was that a stalemate situation soon developed and the men dug themselves in to a trench system, which extended from the Swiss Alps, through northern France, 400 miles to the North Sea. This line of trenches became known as the Western Front. The large scale use of machine guns made defending trench systems much easier than attacking them. The results were to prove devastating on both sides in terms of numbers of men killed, lost and wounded.

Europe (especially France) became the main area of conflict for the entire duration of the war, but, as with the first battle of Ypres (Belgium) in October 1914, the situation escalated into a world war with countries making loose alliances. Japan made alliances with Britain, France and Russia. Turkey and some of the Eastern European countries joined Germany, Austria-Hungary and Italy. The situation was further complicated by power struggles in Africa and South America.

Fighting took place at sea as well as on land. On the lead up to war, there had been an arms build up amongst a number of countries, most notably Germany, which had made a large number of new battleships. The British fleet was still by far the biggest in the world but Germany had closed the gap significantly by 1914. Towards the end of the year, German warships were regularly seen around the English coast, some even bombarded coastal settlements (ie Scarborough, Hartlepool and Whitby were attacked). After a sea battle between the British High Seas Fleet and the German Navy at Dogger Bank in January 1915, German coastal bombardments ceased. The war was to last almost 4 more years. Over 60 million military personnel were mobilised in Europe between 1914 and 1918'.

(Source - BBC History)

British patriotism

Many patriotic postcards were sent by young men who believed they were going on some great adventure, which would be over 'all too soon'. For most, this was not a war of great adventures but a war of degradation and horror, with sights and sounds that few would forget. Many who returned home were much changed in outlook and disposition. Their world would never be the same again.

Whether men survived or died, hit by a shell or shrapnel, or shot by a bullet, was more often than not a straightforward coincidence of time and place.

Charlie Robeson was to become 'one of the lucky ones'.

Patriotic postcards were sent in their thousands

HANDS ACROSS THE SEA. No.

(Authors collection)

"THE DIE IS CAST"

THE DIE IS CAST—
and it is not Peace, for the triumph of might in the world must cease. Too long have the forces of evil prevailed; too long has the terror been unassailed; so those who count freedom a sacred thing have answered the call and the challenging.

It is ours to stand fast to the very end, shoulder to shoulder and friend with friend, stern of soul in the midst of strife for the things that are dearer by far than life—even to those in the flower of youth —Justice and Honour and Freedom and Truth: Pray God that His strong right arm may be our strength on earth; in air and sea!

—*Allan Junior.*

7264

(Authors collection)

" ENGLAND !
WHAT THOU WERT, THOU ART ! "
Henry Newbolt

Young men volunteered in droves in the autumn of 1914. Often the entire male population of a small town would enlist together, forming 'pals battalions'. This method of recruitment soon stopped when casualty figures were posted in the local press.

(Authors collection)

43

The following patriotic poem
was written by Kelso poet,
Will Ogilvie at the outbreak
of war and presented to
children of a Borders School.

Song For The Flag

Blow down, ye winds, from Eildon
And set these folds a-swing!
Shake forth this flag of Empire
To children of the King!
The boldest knees have bowed to it,
The bravest hearts have bled
To guard the royal banner
And hold its wings outspread!

See! Red that burns for courage,
And Blue that shines for truth,
And White that gleams with purity-
Look up, clear eyes of youth!
What homage will ye bring them,
These colours twined and crossed
With old-time grief and glory
And battles won and lost?

No manse so wrapped in moorland,
No farm so far afield,
But owes a son to Empire,
A hand to sword and shield;
No child of all our homesteads
But honour holds him bound
To fight that yonder banner
Rule aye on Border ground.

But till that day shall waken,
And till that need shall call,
Take for your sword the daily task
That fills the hand of all;
For best we build our Empire
And best we serve our King
Who do the simple duty
The passing hour shall bring.

Will Ogilvie, Holefield, Kelso

How Kelso and other Border towns responded at the outbreak of war.

Kelso Volunteers leaving for the war on 7th August 1914 (4 days after war was declared)
Charlie posted this card to Winnie on August 13th 1914, at the outbreak of war. It reads on the back....Kelso Volunteers leaving for France... the nurses are in front (behind the pipe band) with the volunteers at the back.... They marched to Gala!

Men of the National Reserve leaving Kelso on 8th August 1914 (*Alastair Brooks*).

Stobs infantry training camp, Hawick

Cavalry Line, Stobs Camp, Hawick.

(Authors collection)

Stobs farm near Hawick was bought by the Ministry of Defence in 1903 as a summer training camp. It was used by thousands of soldiers. Many Border men trained at Stobs Camp before leaving for the Western Front. Winnie Scott's father trained here in 1914 when he was nearly 50 years old. During WWI, the camp was used as a prisoner of war detention centre for German soldiers.

A 'family day' at Stobs camp in 1906. It is highly likely that many of the 'boys' seen in this photograph would not survive the war, which started 8 years later.

(Authors collection)

Winnie writes to her sister and passes comment about the start of war with Germany.

A postcard sent from Winnie to sister Lil, during the first week of the war on 7th August 1914. It was posted from her family home in Glen Prosen near Forfar, where her father was gamekeeper to the Stormonth Darlings. Britain had declared war with Germany three days earlier on 4th August.

POST CARD

"Ideal" D&S K Series.

Address only to be Written Here

Miss Lily Scott.
Eccles House
Eccles
Kelso.

Winnie's father Alexander Scott volunteered for his local regiment the Black Watch at the outbreak of war. (He is the 3rd soldier from the right hand side).

Over the next four years (1914–18), Winnie and her sisters, Flo and Lil, continued to work in the country houses around Kelso. As the war progressed, the number of injured men requiring treatment increased dramatically. Soon, these houses were converted to hospitals for the treatment of soldiers. Winnie and her sisters became nurses. The continual stream of injured men must have seemed endless.

Postcards through 1914

Teviot Bridge, Kelso.

(Authors collection)

Postcard from Winnie and sister Flo to their sister Lil on 20th August 1914, two weeks after war broke out. They say again how awful the beginning of the war is. Posted in Kirriemuir, on a short visit home to their parents, at Glen Prosen, Forfarshire.

The last few months of peace

KELSO ABBEY AND BRIDGE.

Kelso Bridge.

(Authors collection)

A postcard from Charlie (C.R) to Winnie's sister Lil, who is lying ill in the Edinburgh Royal Infirmary – posted earlier in (May) 1914. Charlie states that he'd been visiting Winnie at Edenbank House (E.B.).

KOSB volunteers leaving Jedburgh for the war

Jedburgh Territorials leaving for France and the Western Front in August 1914. (Alastair Brooks).

Volunteers leaving Hawick

Territorial Army soldiers leaving Hawick in August 1914.
This postcard was sent to Winnie on 15th August 1914. Charlie writes on the back, 'Hawick is very quiet with all the lads away!'

The Regular Army leaves Galashiels for France

Kelso and Jedburgh KOSB leave Galashiels for the Front, August 1914 (Alastair Brooks).

Kelso Railway Station was the focal point for young men leaving the town

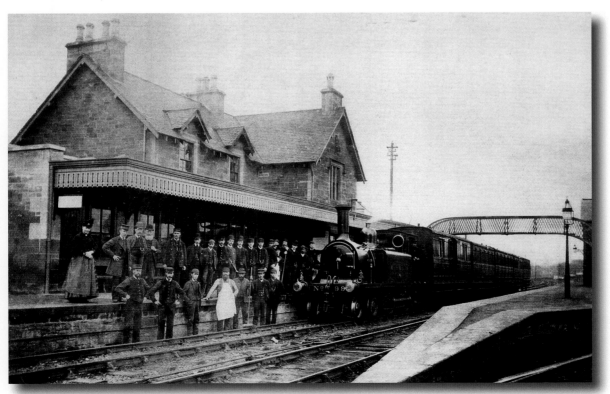

Kelso Station (c.1890). The last sight of Kelso for many men leaving the town would have been from the train to Berwick, for onward recruitment and embarkation.

(Authors collection)

The Main Battlefields of the Western Front from 1914 to 1918.

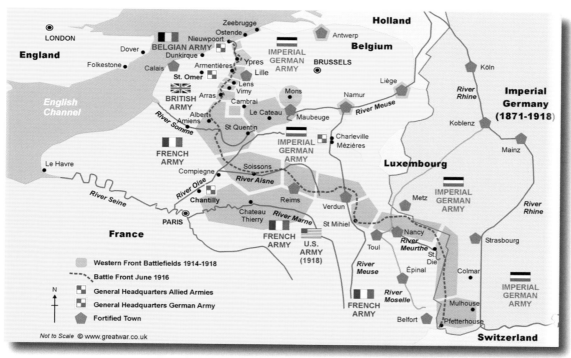

Map showing the positions of the opposing armies along the Western Front during World War 1,
(by kind permission of Joanna Legg www.greatwar.co.uk).

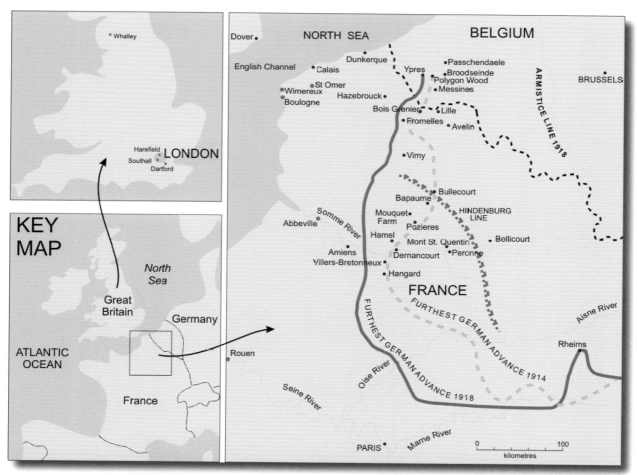

Map showing the main British battlefield areas during World War 1, in northern France (Somme) and Belgium
(Ypres and Passchendaele), www.greatwar.co.uk.

The year 1915 and Stalemate on the Western Front

The war in France and Belgium

Because the war during 1914 had become a stalemate along a trench system extending to over 400 miles, there was no way an opposing army could get around it to outflank the enemy. A move by one side was followed by a tactical move on the opposing side, with the result that many local battles broke out. The British Army had engaged the enemy in a significant number of major battles during 1914, but by the end of the year a complete deadlock had occurred and a siege situation developed. There were extended periods during the war, lasting several months, when fighting on a major scale abated. This allowed each side to rest, to develop new tactics and to train more men, for the next major offensive.

'By the end of November 1914 in France and by the end of the first Battles of Ypres in Belgium, the armies of both sides were completely entrenched. By early 1915, the British Army had become greatly outnumbered and out gunned. It was clear that a new approach was required if progress was to be made. New technologies were developed: the flame thrower, the use of gas (both mustard gas and chlorine gas) and ever more powerful machine guns, mortars and grenades. Major battles were fought during 1915, including the second Battle of Ypres in Belgium in April and May and the Battle of Loos in northern France in September and October.

The British government had not been prepared for war in 1914 and the army complained that it had insufficient supplies and equipment. General discontent amongst the civilian population led to the formation of a coalition government in May of 1915. By October, women were being recruited to undertake traditional men's work, such as driving trains and buses and working heavy factory machinery. The war was not over by Christmas 1914, as many had thought. It became clear that it was going to be a very long, expensive and bloody war of attrition. The entire war effort had to be re-thought by the government and they negotiated new loans from the United States of America. They updated and amended the Defence of the Realm Act which gave them the legal power to censor the press, requisition property and control worker's jobs, pay and conditions. Much of Britain's food was imported and there was a concerted effort to grow more at home, to reduce food dependency from other countries.

In northern France and Belgium, and all along the Western Front, the stalemate continued. Thousands of men fought and died, with very little achieved by way of ground taken. The battles fought were generally inconclusive. Farmland turned to quagmire and the battlefields became scenes of desolation, where nothing grew and only rats and foxes (and men) eked out a miserable existence. Italy joined the war and from April 1915 fought with the Allied forces. A new front was opened in Turkey at the Gallipoli peninsula in April 1915, spearheaded by the British and the French. It was Australian and New Zealand (ANZAC) forces that made up the bulk of the army at Gallipoli. Although the Gallipoli campaign continued for nine months, little was achieved and in January 1916, the much reduced Allied forces withdrew from the area. The Campaign had been a failure.'

'Naval skirmishes increased during 1915 but Britain used her powerful navy to keep the bulk of enemy ships tied down in port. Germany began to suffer materials, equipment and food shortages. In response, Germany increased her submarine fleet and began a concerted effort to destroy Allied merchant and naval shipping. Submarines were used very effectively for the first time during WWI and on the 7th May the Lusitania, a luxury passenger liner travelling from the United States, was sunk off the south coast of Ireland. Almost 1,200 civilians were drowned, including over 100 Americans. Normally during wartime, large ships travelled in a zig-zag pattern, to make them more difficult to attack. The Lusitania was sailing a direct course, which made her an easy target. She sank very quickly. Following the sinking, the German fleet withdrew to port, afraid that a continued campaign might bring the neutral Americans into the war (which it did), on the side of the British and French.

World War I was the first true world war. The war was conducted on land, sea and for the first time, in the air. On 31st May 1915, London experienced its first attack from the air, as bombs were dropped from German Zeppelin airships. Damage was considerable and during the period 1915-1918, over 2,000 civilians were killed by air raids.'

(Source - BBC History)

The Kings Own Scottish Borderers (KOSB) had a significant role to play at Gallipoli. Their numbers were heavily depleted by the style of warfare experienced and many Borderers lie buried there. The Turks were a very formidable enemy and Allied forces were pinned down on the beaches and lower slopes of the Gallipoli peninsula as they attacked from the sea. This unfortunate situation was to repeat itself 29 years later, (albeit over a much shorter time-span) and suffered by American troops, on Omaha Beach, as part of the D-Day landings, on the 6th of June 1944, during World War II.

Throughout 1915 Charlie was still under contract to Oldham playing professional Rugby League (centre left).　　(Authors collection)

By the autumn of 1915, the regular army, 'the old contemptibles' was becoming depleted. More volunteers, were required, forming 'the new army'

Daily Mail WAR PICTURES

6. THE WORCESTERS GOING INTO ACTION.

OFFICIAL PHOTOGRAPH,
CROWN COPYRIGHT RESERVED.

Despite no significant progress towards winning the war on the Western Front, British resolve remained strong throughout 1915. (IWM).

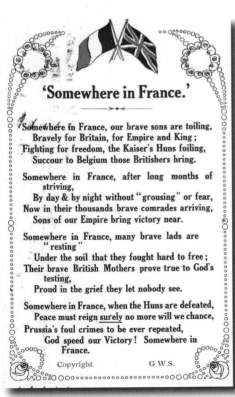

'Somewhere in France.'

Somewhere in France, our brave sons are toiling,
 Bravely for Britain, for Empire and King;
Fighting for freedom, the Kaiser's Huns foiling,
 Succour to Belgium those Britishers bring.

Somewhere in France, after long months of
 striving,
 By day & by night without "grousing" or fear,
Now in their thousands brave comrades arriving,
 Sons of our Empire bring victory near.

Somewhere in France, many brave lads are
 "resting"
 Under the soil that they fought hard to free;
Their brave British Mothers prove true to God's
 testing,
 Proud in the grief they let nobody see.

Somewhere in France, when the Huns are defeated,
 Peace must reign surely no more will we chance,
Prussia's foul crimes to be ever repeated,
 God speed our Victory! Somewhere in
 France.

Copyright.   G.W.S.

*Patriotic postcards were very good at spurring
the troops on.*   (Authors collection)

*Charlie (in boater)
visiting an army
friend in Berwick on
Tweed in 1915.*

(Authors collection)

CHARGE!

"Scotland for ever."

It's Our Flag

Fight for it
Work for it

WW1 morale (Authors collection)
boosting image.

WWI postcard appealing for recruits, but for so many (Authors collection)
young men, Scotland was never seen again!

1915 was the worst year for the Kings Own Scottish Borderers

The 1/4th Battalion Kings Own Scottish Borderers (KOSB) under the command of Major A Stevenson, on parade in Shedden Park Kelso to mark the Coronation of George V in June 1911. Many of these young men would be sent to the Gallipoli peninsula four years later. The oak tree being planted next to the old Park Keepers Lodge still grows in the park today.

A photograph of Officers of the 1/4th Battalion KOSB (May 1915) (Both images from the War Record of the 4th Battalion KOSB).

Charlie had many friends fighting with 'The Borderers' during 1915. The following pages serve as a graphic reminder of the high price the Borderers paid in terms of lives lost (for the most part in a single day), by one Battalion of the KOSB in the Great War, 12th July 1915, during the Gallipoli Campaign in Turkey. This was the worst day in the KOSB's long history of battle honours.

Combined 1915 and Gallipoli Campaign casualty list

(Extracted from *'For King and Country and the Scottish Borderers'* by Gavin Richardson 1987, with additional information from the *'War Record of the 4th Battalion KOSB and Lothian and Border Horse'* 1920, with thanks.)

1/4th (Border) Battalion K.O.S.B. Roll of Honour

The following list includes all officers and other ranks of the 1/4th (Border) Battalion K.O.S.B. who were serving with their unit and became casualties whilst on active service in 1915. Those who died in hospital of wounds or disease were mostly buried at Alexandria in Egypt or at Malta. Some died *en route* to hospital and were buried at sea. Very few who were killed in action and were buried on the Gallipoli Peninsula have marked graves today. The regimental identification numbers under 1,000 signify that they were issued before the outbreak of war in August 1914 and belonged to those who were members of the 4th Battalion K.O.S.B. (Territorial Force). In some cases they go back to 1908 when the Territorial Force was inaugurated. Later on in the war all the men received new numbers starting at 200,000.

The place name after each surname in the "other ranks" section, represents place of birth. The old county names are used and are abbreviated as follows;

Ang. = Angus	Kin. = Kincardineshire
Ant. = Antrim	Kir. = Kirkcudbrightshire
Arg. = Argyllshire	Lan. = Lanarkshire
Ber. = Berwickshire	Midx. = Middlesex
Caith. = Caithness	Mid. = Midlothian
Cla. = Clackmannanshire	Nor. = Northumberland
Cork. = Cork	Peeb. = Peeblesshire
Cum. = Cumberland	Per. = Perthshire
Dum. = Dumfriesshire	Penn. = Pennsylvania, U.S.A.
Dub. = Dublin	Rox. = Roxburghshire
For. = Forfarshire	Sel. = Selkirkshire
Had. = Haddingtonshire	Sur. = Surrey
Hants. = Hampshire	Wig. = Wigtownshire
Kil. = Kildare	York. = Yorkshire

KOSB cap badge.

Officers

Lt.-Col. J. McNeile	Missing, death accepted	12/ 7/15
Maj. J. Herbertson	Missing, death accepted	12/ 7/15
Surg.-Maj. D. R. Taylor, R.A.M.C. (att. K.O.S.B.)	Killed in action	12/ 7/15
Capt. and Adjutant J. C. Lang	Missing, death accepted	12/ 7/15
Capt. H. Sanderson	Missing, death accepted	12/ 7/15
Capt. A. Wallace	Killed in action	12/ 7/15
Lieut. T. M. Alexander	Killed in action	12/ 7/15
Lieut. A. Bulman	Missing, death accepted	12/ 7/15
Lieut. J. B. Innes	Killed in action	12/ 7/15
Lieut. P. Woodhead	Missing, death accepted	12/ 7/15
2nd. Lieut. A. H. M. Henderson	Killed in action	12/ 7/15
2nd. Lieut. J. B. Patrick	Missing, death accepted	12/ 7/15
2nd. Lieut. J. A. G. Cairns	Killed in action	29/12/15

Other Ranks

4462	Pte.	Cowe, R., Duns, Ber.	Killed in action	24/ 6/15
6901	Pte.	Crombie, J., Ladhope, Sel.	Died of wounds	28/ 6/15
6694	Pte.	Dick, J., Melrose, Rox.	Died of wounds	20/ 6/15
843	Pte.	Fairgrieve, J., Kelso, Rox.	Died of wounds	18/ 6/15
4451	L./Cpl.	Ford, J., Coldstream, Ber.	Killed in action	24/ 6/15
7126	Pte.	Kinghorn, W., Duns, Ber.	Died of wounds	21/ 6/15
7106	Pte.	Lindores, A., Earlston, Ber.	Died of wounds	22/ 6/15
6498	Pte.	Murray, J., Selkirk, Sel.	Died of wounds	21/ 6/15
564	Cpl.	Stevenson, T., Hawick, Rox.	Died of wounds	1/ 7/15
6658	Pte.	Amos, J., Galashiels, Sel.	Missing, presumed dead	12/ 7/15
7480	Pte.	Anderson, G., Boghall, Mid.	Missing, presumed dead	12/ 7/15
7139	Pte.	Allan, D., Dundee, Ang.	Missing, presumed dead	12/ 7/15
6902	Pte.	Andison, J., Galashiels, Sel.	Killed in action	12/ 7/15
7433	Pte.	Amos, H., Hawick, Rox.	Killed in action	12/ 7/15
7310	Pte.	Aikman, A., Cockburnspath, Ber.	Missing, presumed dead	12/ 7/15
6775	Pte.	Anderson, J., Roxburgh, Rox.	Missing, presumed dead	12/ 7/15
4371	Sgt.	Aikman, W., Galashiels, Sel.	Missing, presumed dead	12/ 7/15
6790	Pte.	Angus, H., Partick, Lan.	Missing, presumed dead	12/ 7/15
7619	Pte.	Anderson, F., Duns, Ber.	Missing, presumed dead	12/ 7/15
7582	Pte.	Anderson, A., Duns, Ber.	Missing, presumed dead	12/ 7/15
494	L./Cpl.	Anderson, C., Hawick, Rox.	Missing, presumed dead	12/ 7/15
6484	Pte.	Brydone, A., Selkirk, Sel.	Missing, presumed dead	12/ 7/15
6494	Pte.	Ballantyne, J., Selkirk, Sel.	Missing, presumed dead	12/ 7/15
6717	L./Cpl.	Brown, H., Stow, Mid.	Missing, presumed dead	12/ 7/15
785	Pte.	Bunyan, A., Melrose, Rox.	Missing, presumed dead	12/ 7/15
6880	Pte.	Bennett, W., Galashiels, Sel.	Missing, presumed dead	12/ 7/15
7654	Pte.	Beattie, J., Hawick, Rox.	Missing, presumed dead	12/ 7/15

7362	Pte.	Brown, P., Eyemouth, Ber.	Missing, presumed dead	12/ 7/15
7142	Pte.	Best, A., Woodhouse, Rox.	Missing, presumed dead	12/ 7/15
7553	Pte.	Bookless, W., Swinton, Ber.	Killed in action	12/ 7/15
6897	Pte.	Barbour, G., Galashiels, Sel.	Killed in action	12/ 7/15
6854	Pte.	Brown, A., Stow, Mid.	Killed in action	12/ 7/15
7192	Pte.	Ballantyne, G., Galashiels, Sel.	Killed in action	12/ 7/15
7305	Pte.	Brown, R., Selkirk, Sel.	Killed in action	12/ 7/15
917	Pte.	Beatson, W., Ancrum, Rox.	Killed in action	12/ 7/15
573	Pte.	Blain, J., Newton Stewart, Wig.	Missing, presumed dead	12/ 7/15
7464	Pte.	Boyd, G., Hawick, Rox.	Missing, presumed dead	12/ 7/15
7449	L./Cpl.	Ballantyne, J., Crailing, Rox.	Missing, presumed dead	12/ 7/15
7622	Pte.	Buckham, A., Synton, Sel.	Missing, presumed dead	12/ 7/15
7583	Pte.	Barnett, W., Dunbar, Had.	Missing, presumed dead	12/ 7/15
699	Pte.	Barrett, W., Hawick, Rox.	Missing, presumed dead	12/ 7/15
6732	Pte.	Currie, J., Selkirk, Sel.	Missing, presumed dead	12/ 7/15
6666	Pte.	Cockburn, G., Galashiels, Sel.	Missing, presumed dead	12/ 7/15
6861	Pte.	Clark, T., Darnick, Rox.	Missing, presumed dead	12/ 7/15
6892	Pte.	Cranston, W., Hawick, Rox.	Missing, presumed dead	12/ 7/15
6988	Pte.	Coughlin, J., Hawick, Rox.	Missing, presumed dead	12/ 7/15
7095	Pte.	Clelland, W., Galashiels, Sel.	Missing, presumed dead	12/ 7/15
7148	Pte.	Cairns, G., Hownam, Rox.	Missing, presumed dead	12/ 7/15
4039	Cpl.	Clapham, R., Dunbar, Had.	Killed in action	12/ 7/15
6723	Pte.	Currie, J., Selkirk, Sel.	Killed in action	12/ 7/15
6898	Pte.	Cameron, R., Galashiels, Sel.	Killed in action	12/ 7/15
7197	Pte.	Callander, F., Forfar, For.	Killed in action	12/ 7/15
7404	Pte.	Cuthill, S., Hawick, Rox.	Killed in action	12/ 7/15
491	Pte.	Cunningham, E., Hawick, Rox.	Killed in action	12/ 7/15
629	Pte.	Combe, W., Hawick, Rox.	Died of wounds	12/ 7/15
7306	Pte.	Chalmers, W., Kirkcudbright, Kir.	Missing, presumed dead	12/ 7/15
6748	Pte.	Cessford, A., Lauder, Ber.	Missing, presumed dead	12/ 7/15
899	Pte.	Cranston, A., Jedburgh, Rox.	Missing, presumed dead	12/ 7/15
918	Cpl.	Caldwell, A., Hawick, Rox.	Missing, presumed dead	12/ 7/15
6826	Pte.	Cairns, W., Hawick, Rox.	Missing, presumed dead	12/ 7/15
6818	Pte.	Cunningham, A., Hawick, Rox.	Missing, presumed dead	12/ 7/15
6529	Pte.	Cowan, W., Galashiels, Sel.	Missing, presumed dead	12/ 7/15
6542	Pte.	Chisholm, R., Selkirk, Sel.	Missing, presumed dead	12/ 7/15
6491	Pte.	Dalgliesh, A., Kirkhope, Sel.	Missing, presumed dead	12/ 7/15
6874	Pte.	Dalgliesh, J., Cornhill, Nor.	Missing, presumed dead	12/ 7/15
7030	Pte.	Deans, J., Westruther, Ber.	Missing, presumed dead	12/ 7/15
7217	Pte.	Doherty, J., Roxburghshire	Missing, presumed dead	12/ 7/15
7285	Pte.	Darrie, J., Berwickshire	Missing, presumed dead	12/ 7/15
6619	Pte.	Davidson, A., Galashiels, Sel.	Killed in action	12/ 7/15
4274	Cpl.	Dods, W., Newcastle, Nor.	Killed in action	12/ 7/15
6815	Pte.	Davidson, R., Roberton, Rox.	Killed in action	12/ 7/15
339	Pte.	Douglas, J., Wilton, Rox.	Killed in action	12/ 7/15
7252	Pte.	Dodds, R., Abbey St. Bathans, Ber.	Missing, presumed dead	12/ 7/15
760	Pte.	Davidson, G., Stichill, Rox.	Missing, presumed dead	12/ 7/15
900	Pte.	Dickson, R., Jedburgh, Rox.	Missing, presumed dead	12/ 7/15
554	Pte.	Darling, W., Melrose, Rox.	Missing, presumed dead	12/ 7/15
6467	Pte.	Delaney, D., Athy, Kil.	Missing, presumed dead	12/ 7/15

7736	Pte.	Douglas, T., Selkirk, Sel.	Missing, presumed dead	12/ 7/15
7601	Pte.	Darling, J., Duns, Ber.	Missing, presumed dead	12/ 7/15
446	Pte.	Drummond, A., Hobkirk, Rox.	Missing, presumed dead	12/ 7/15
6794	Pte.	Edgar, J., Cummertrees, Dum.	Missing, presumed dead	12/ 7/15
6835	Pte.	Eckford, R., Cornhill, Nor.	Missing, presumed dead	12/ 7/15
7387	Pte.	Emslie, W., Eyemouth, Ber.	Missing, presumed dead	12/ 7/15
4339	Pte.	Fairbairn, W., Coldstream, Ber.	Missing, presumed dead	12/ 7/15
4388	L./Cpl.	Frater, J., Ayton, Ber.	Killed in action	12/ 7/15
6589	Pte.	Fox, J., Ayr, Ayrshire	Killed in action	12/ 7/15
6816	Pte.	Forster, J., Nichol Forest, Cum.	Killed in action	12/ 7/15
623	Pte.	Fair, A., Kelso, Rox.	Missing, presumed dead	12/ 7/15
879	Cpl.	Fraser, G., Hawick, Rox.	Missing, presumed dead	12/ 7/15
883	Pte.	Farmer, T., Hawick, Rox.	Missing, presumed dead	12/ 7/15
6466	Pte.	Gall, A., Selkirk, Sel.	Missing, presumed dead	12/ 7/15
6397	Pte.	Grieve, R., Ettrickbridgend, Sel.	Missing, presumed dead	12/ 7/15
782	Pte.	Gilholm, J., Melrose, Rox.	Missing, presumed dead	12/ 7/15
7367	Pte.	Galbraith, J., Edinburgh, Mid.	Missing, presumed dead	12/ 7/15
7314	Pte.	Grant, R., Newcastleton, Rox.	Missing, presumed dead	12/ 7/15
858	Pte.	Gray, A., Kelso, Rox.	Missing, presumed dead	12/ 7/15
4414	Cpl.	Galbraith, J., Swinton, Ber.	Missing, presumed dead	12/ 7/15
7407	Pte.	Grieve, W., Ettrickbridge, Sel.	Missing, presumed dead	12/ 7/15
7542	Pte.	Gladstone, W., Ayton, Ber.	Missing, presumed dead	12/ 7/15
6559	Pte.	Hall, F., Galashiels, Sel.	Missing, presumed dead	12/ 7/15
6511	Pte.	Hardie, J., Galashiels, Sel.	Missing, presumed dead	12/ 7/15
6725	A/L/Cpl.	Hume, G., Walkerburn, Peeb.	Missing, presumed dead	12/ 7/15
6720	Cpl.	Hogg, W., Selkirk, Sel.	Missing, presumed dead	12/ 7/15
4539	Pte.	Hardie, J., Selkirk, Sel.	Missing, presumed dead	12/ 7/15
6844	Pte.	Haig, W., Jedburgh, Rox.	Missing, presumed dead	12/ 7/15
7344	Pte.	Hope, T., Ancrum, Rox.	Missing, presumed dead	12/ 7/15
6519	Pte.	Hill, W., Selkirk, Sel.	Killed in action	12/ 7/15
6652	Pte.	Henderson, A., Glasgow, Lan.	Killed in action	12/ 7/15
6904	Pte.	Handyside, R., Hawick, Rox.	Killed in action	12/ 7/15
7368	Pte.	Hunter, D., Reston, Ber.	Killed in action	12/ 7/15
523	Pte.	Halley, J., Wilton, Rox.	Killed in action	12/ 7/15
7288	Pte.	Hardy, J., Roxburghshire	Missing, presumed dead	12/ 7/15
7291	Pte.	Hall, R., Wooler, Nor.	Missing, presumed dead	12/ 7/15
7259	Pte.	Hume, J., Whitsome, Ber.	Missing, presumed dead	12/ 7/15
6767	Pte.	Hollands, G., Jedburgh, Rox.	Missing, presumed dead	12/ 7/15
6777	Pte.	Hunter, W., Melrose, Rox.	Missing, presumed dead	12/ 7/15
4376	Pte.	Harper, D., Duns, Ber.	Missing, presumed dead	12/ 7/15
4380	Pte.	Haig, A., Croydon, Sur.	Missing, presumed dead	12/ 7/15
857	Pte.	Haig, R., Jedburgh, Rox.	Missing, presumed dead	12/ 7/15
822	Pte.	Hendry, A., Greenlaw, Ber.	Missing, presumed dead	12/ 7/15
844	A/L/Cpl.	Heggie, A., Wilton, Rox.	Missing, presumed dead	12/ 7/15
4446	Pte.	Hunter, W., Duns, Ber.	Missing, presumed dead	12/ 7/15
892	Pte.	Halliday, R., Hawick, Rox.	Missing, presumed dead	12/ 7/15
659	Pte.	Hesketh, G., Hamilton, Lan.	Missing, presumed dead	12/ 7/15
106	Pte.	Hogarth, A., Kelso, Rox.	Missing, presumed dead	12/ 7/15
553	Pte.	Hunter, J., Jedburgh, Rox.	Missing, presumed dead	12/ 7/15
6798	Pte.	Hogg, J., Mertoun, Rox.	Missing, presumed dead	12/ 7/15

6454	Pte.	Henderson, A., Selkirk, Sel.	Missing, presumed dead	12/ 7/15
7438	Pte.	Hendry, J., Mordington, Ber.	Missing, presumed dead	12/ 7/15
678	Pte.	Hogg, W., Wilton, Rox.	Missing, presumed dead	12/ 7/15
477	Pte.	Hall, C., Hawick, Rox.	Missing, presumed dead	12/ 7/15
4452	Pte.	Hope, W., Coldingham, Ber.	Missing, presumed dead	12/ 7/15
6770	Pte.	Herkes, W., Coldstream, Ber.	Missing, presumed dead	12/ 7/15
6508	Pte.	Imrie, H., Galashiels, Sel.	Missing, presumed dead	12/ 7/15
6717	Pte.	Inglis, G., Chirnside, Ber.	Missing, presumed dead	12/ 7/15
6586	A/L/Cpl.	Johnston, W., Selkirk, Sel.	Missing, presumed dead	12/ 7/15
7466	Pte.	Jamieson, D., Gordon, Ber.	Missing, presumed dead	12/ 7/15
4020	Sgt.	Johnstone, W., Harbridge, Hants.	Missing, presumed dead	12/ 7/15
7058	Pte.	Johnston, G., Innerwick, Had.	Missing, presumed dead	12/ 7/15
6473	Pte.	Johnstone, A., Galashiels, Sel.	Missing, presumed dead	12/ 7/15
7459	Pte.	Jeffrey, W., Glasgow, Lan.	Missing, presumed dead	12/ 7/15
448	Pte.	Jackson, H., Leeds, Yor.	Missing, presumed dead	12/ 7/15
6830	Pte.	Keddie, C., Galashiels, Sel.	Missing, presumed dead	12/ 7/15
6599	Pte.	Knox, A., Newcastle, Nor.	Killed in action	12/ 7/15
779	Pte.	Kerr, J., Swinton, Ber.	Killed in action	12/ 7/15
7345	Pte.	Kerr, G., Edrom, Ber.	Killed in action	12/ 7/15
6779	Pte.	Kinnon, J., Yarrow, Sel.	Killed in action	12/ 7/15
895	Pte.	Knox, J., Kelso, Rox.	Missing, presumed dead	12/ 7/15
745	Pte.	Kennedy, J., Dumfries, Dum.	Missing, presumed dead	12/ 7/15
726	Pte.	Kerr, J., Wilton, Rox.	Missing, presumed dead	12/ 7/15
6561	Pte.	Laing, R., Galashiels, Sel.	Missing, presumed dead	12/ 7/15
818	Pte.	Law, J., Langholm, Dum.	Missing, presumed dead	12/ 7/15
7573	L./Cpl.	Ludski, N., Leeds, Yor.	Missing, presumed dead	12/ 7/15
6839	Pte.	Lunn, T., Galashiels, Sel.	Missing, presumed dead	12/ 7/15
7227	Pte.	Leitch, J., Duns, Ber.	Missing, presumed dead	12/ 7/15
7077	Pte.	Lorimer, A., Eccles, Ber.	Killed in action	12/ 7/15
844	Cpl.	Lawson, T., Ancrum, Rox.	Killed in action	12/ 7/15
885	Pte.	Laidlaw, T., Jedburgh, Rox.	Missing, presumed dead	12/ 7/15
7372	Pte.	Morley, S., Hawick, Rox.	Missing, presumed dead	12/ 7/15
6610	Pte.	McCulloch, C., Hawick, Rox.	Missing, presumed dead	12/ 7/15
6026	Sgt.	Millar, D., Galashiels, Sel.	Missing, presumed dead	12/ 7/15
7165	Pte.	Mather, J., Kelso, Rox.	Missing, presumed dead	12/ 7/15
7668	Pte.	Mack, A., Galashiels, Sel.	Killed in action	12/ 7/15
7060	Pte.	Millar, W., Galashiels, Sel.	Killed in action	12/ 7/15
7238	Pte.	Mack, W., Duns, Ber.	Missing, presumed dead	12/ 7/15
6766	L./Cpl.	Martin, A., Coldingham, Ber.	Missing, presumed dead	12/ 7/15
7232	Pte.	Muir, M., Beith, Ayr.	Missing, presumed dead	12/ 7/15
6423	L./Sgt.	Millar, R., Selkirk, Sel.	Missing, presumed dead	12/ 7/15
4403	Pte.	Marshall, H., Cornhill, Nor.	Missing, presumed dead	12/ 7/15
757	Pte.	Mackenzie, J., Ramshope, Nor.	Missing, presumed dead	12/ 7/15
580	Sgt.	McPherson, J., Jedburgh, Rox.	Missing, presumed dead	12/ 7/15
598	Pte.	Messer, A., Galashiels, Sel.	Missing, presumed dead	12/ 7/15
633	Pte.	Myles, J., Hawick, Rox.	Missing, presumed dead	12/ 7/15
657	Pte.	Murray, J., Hawick, Rox.	Missing, presumed dead	12/ 7/15
53	Sgt.	Middlemas, A., Kelso, Rox.	Missing, presumed dead	12/ 7/15
6802	Pte.	McTavish, F., Fogo, Ber.	Missing, presumed dead	12/ 7/15
6457	Pte.	Miller, J., Selkirk, Sel.	Missing, presumed dead	12/ 7/15

7447	Pte.	Minto, P., Jedburgh, Rox.	Missing, presumed dead	12/ 7/15
7425	Pte.	Mason, R., Morvern, Arg.	Missing, presumed dead	12/ 7/15
527	Cpl.	Murray, J., Kelso, Rox.	Missing, presumed dead	12/ 7/15
545	Cpl.	Neil, W., Kelso, Rox.	Missing, presumed dead	12/ 7/15
7439	Pte.	Nairn, W., Coldingham, Ber.	Killed in action	12/ 7/15
6864	Pte.	Oag, D., Thurso, Caith.	Missing, presumed dead	12/ 7/15
7078	Pte.	Oliver, P., Galashiels, Sel.	Killed in action	12/ 7/15
617	L./Sgt.	Oliver, J., Jedburgh, Rox.	Missing, presumed dead	12/ 7/15
6781	Pte.	Paterson, W., Leadhills, Lan.	Missing, presumed dead	12/ 7/15
7321	Pte.	Paterson, J., Westruther, Ber.	Missing, presumed dead	12/ 7/15
7265	Pte.	Purves, A., Edrom, Ber.	Missing, presumed dead	12/ 7/15
6574	Pte.	Paton, W., Galashiels, Sel.	Died of wounds	12/ 7/15
6685	L./Cpl.	Poustie, J., Galashiels, Sel.	Missing, presumed dead	12/ 7/15
6719	Pte.	Paterson, R., Galashiels, Sel.	Missing, presumed dead	12/ 7/15
6646	Pte.	Pringle, G., Galashiels, Sel.	Missing, presumed dead	12/ 7/15
781	Pte.	Polwarth, T., Duns, Ber.	Missing, presumed dead	12/ 7/15
7108	Pte.	Piercy, G., Cornhill, Nor.	Missing, presumed dead	12/ 7/15
7169	Pte.	Queenan, J., Jedburgh, Rox.	Missing, presumed dead	12/ 7/15
7235	Pte.	Quinn, A., Swinton, Ber.	Missing, presumed dead	12/ 7/15
6485	Pte.	Reid, A., Selkirk, Sel.	Missing, presumed dead	12/ 7/15
6675	L./Cpl.	Reid, A., Selkirk, Sel.	Missing, presumed dead	12/ 7/15
6137	L./Cpl.	Redpath, R., Galashiels, Sel.	Missing, presumed dead	12/ 7/15
4485	Pte.	Rutherford, A., Stow, Mid.	Missing, presumed dead	12/ 7/15
7724	Pte.	Ritchie, D., Eyemouth, Ber.	Missing, presumed dead	12/ 7/15
7036	Pte.	Rutherford, W., Selkirk, Sel.	Missing, presumed dead	12/ 7/15
7046	L./Cpl.	Rathie, W., Bowhill, Sel.	Missing, presumed dead	12/ 7/15
6997	Pte.	Rutherford, W., Melrose, Rox.	Missing, presumed dead	12/ 7/15
6911	Pte.	Riddle, R., Galashiels, Sel.	Missing, presumed dead	12/ 7/15
7172	Pte.	Robertson, J., Morebattle, Rox.	Missing, presumed dead	12/ 7/15
7275	Pte.	Richley, W., Newcastle, Nor.	Missing, presumed dead	12/ 7/15
6722	A./Cpl.	Rae, J., Govan, Lan.	Killed in action	12/ 7/15
6912	Pte.	Riddle, W., Galashiels, Sel.	Killed in action	12/ 7/15
6924	Pte.	Rutherford, G., Hawick, Rox.	Killed in action	12/ 7/15
7519	Pte.	Richardson, J., Kelso, Rox.	Killed in action	12/ 7/15
643	Pte.	Reid, W., Hawick, Rox.	Missing, presumed dead	12/ 7/15
749	Pte.	Rae, J., Hawick, Rox.	Missing, presumed dead	12/ 7/15
6807	Pte.	Romanis, T., Galashiels, Sel.	Missing, presumed dead	12/ 7/15
6532	L./Cpl.	Russell, A., Hawick, Rox.	Missing, presumed dead	12/ 7/15
6439	Pte.	Roden, H., Selkirk, Sel.	Missing, presumed dead	12/ 7/15
7461	Pte.	Rutherford, T., Hawick, Rox.	Missing, presumed dead	12/ 7/15
7415	Pte.	Rae, W., Hawick, Rox.	Missing, presumed dead	12/ 7/15
496	Pte.	Rodger, W., Hawick, Rox.	Missing, presumed dead	12/ 7/15
515	Pte.	Rose, J., Belfast, Ant.	Missing, presumed dead	12/ 7/15
4459	L./Cpl.	Robertson, A., Duns, Ber.	Missing, presumed dead	12/ 7/15
7357	Pte.	Sword, A., Midlem, Rox.	Missing, presumed dead	12/ 7/15
6478	Pte.	Stewart, W., Selkirk, Sel.	Missing, presumed dead	12/ 7/15
6703	Cpl.	Sanderson, T., Galashiels, Sel.	Missing, presumed dead	12/ 7/15
6389	L./Cpl.	Scott, W., Galashiels, Sel.	Missing, presumed dead	12/ 7/15
4550	Pte.	Spalding, G., Hawick, Rox.	Missing, presumed dead	12/ 7/15
784	Pte.	Stewart, W., Melrose, Rox.	Missing, presumed dead	12/ 7/15

6890	Pte.	Smith, G., Jedburgh, Rox.	Missing, presumed dead	12/ 7/15
7007	Pte.	Snowden, J., Galashiels, Sel.	Missing, presumed dead	12/ 7/15
6981	Pte.	Shiel, J., Melrose, Rox.	Missing, presumed dead	12/ 7/15
7000	Pte.	Sanderson, T., Roxburghshire	Missing, presumed dead	12/ 7/15
7062	Pte.	Smellie, J., Cork, Cork.	Missing, presumed dead	12/ 7/15
7270	Pte.	Scott, A., Hawick, Rox.	Missing, presumed dead	12/ 7/15
6171	Sgt.	Scott, J., Galashiels, Sel.	Missing, presumed dead	12/ 7/15
7555	Pte.	Sanderson, W., Norham, Nor.	Missing, presumed dead	12/ 7/15
7239	Pte.	Smart, J., Galashiels, Sel.	Killed in action	12/ 7/15
6772	Pte.	Sanderson, J., Galashiels, Sel.	Missing, presumed dead	12/ 7/15
7242	Pte.	Simpson, R., Selkirk, Sel.	Missing, presumed dead	12/ 7/15
6425	L./Cpl.	Smith, J., Aberlady, Had.	Missing, presumed dead	12/ 7/15
4354	Pte.	Scott, W., Greenlaw, Ber.	Missing, presumed dead	12/ 7/15
897	Pte.	Scott, W., Hawick, Rox.	Missing, presumed dead	12/ 7/15
574	Pte.	Storrie, J., Jedburgh, Rox.	Missing, presumed dead	12/ 7/15
306	Pte.	Street, C., Kelso, Rox.	Missing, presumed dead	12/ 7/15
6762	Pte.	Smail, A., Hawick, Rox.	Missing, presumed dead	12/ 7/15
6808	Pte.	Scott, W., Galashiels, Sel.	Killed in action	12/ 7/15
6819	Cpl.	Smith, W., Hawick, Rox.	Missing, presumed dead	12/ 7/15
6471	Pte.	Stevenson, J., Edinburgh, Mid.	Missing, presumed dead	12/ 7/15
7378	Pte.	Shearlaw, A., Ayton, Ber.	Missing, presumed dead	12/ 7/15
7443	Pte.	Schooler, W., Spittal, Nor.	Missing, presumed dead	12/ 7/15
7430	Pte.	Swanston, P., Gordon, Ber.	Missing, presumed dead	12/ 7/15
7580	Pte.	Sligh, R., Galashiels, Sel.	Missing, presumed dead	12/ 7/15
674	Pte.	Storrie, A., Lilliesleaf, Rox.	Missing, presumed dead	12/ 7/15
697	Pte.	Stewart, D., Hawick, Rox.	Missing, presumed dead	12/ 7/15
540	Pte.	Stavert, R., Duns, Ber.	Missing, presumed dead	12/ 7/15
516	Pte.	Scott, M., Hawick, Rox.	Missing, presumed dead	12/ 7/15
488	Pte.	Scott, W., Caddonfoot, Sel.	Missing, presumed dead	12/ 7/15
7241	Pte.	Scott, G., Duns, Ber.	Died of wounds	12/ 7/15
6500	Pte.	Tait, J., Hawick, Rox.	Missing, presumed dead	12/ 7/15
4518	Pte.	Thomson, G., Philadelphia, Pen., USA	Missing, presumed dead	12/ 7/15
4519	Pte.	Townsley, M., Tweedmouth, Nor.	Missing, presumed dead	12/ 7/15
6727	Pte.	Thomson, T., Innerleithen, Peeb.	Missing, presumed dead	12/ 7/15
6983	Pte.	Tyson, J., Selkirk, Sel.	Missing, presumed dead	12/ 7/15
7359	Pte.	Telfer, J., Hownam, Rox.	Missing, presumed dead	12/ 7/15
7300	Pte.	Thomson, A., Southdean, Rox.	Missing, presumed dead	12/ 7/15
7301	Pte.	Telfer, A., Fairloans, Rox.	Missing, presumed dead	12/ 7/15
570	Sgt.	Thomson, W., Melrose, Rox.	Missing, presumed dead	12/ 7/15
656	Pte.	Thomson, W., Wilton, Rox.	Missing, presumed dead	12/ 7/15
7402	Pte.	Turnbull, T., Gordon, Ber.	Missing, presumed dead	12/ 7/15
7416	Pte.	Thomson, T., Hawick, Rox.	Missing, presumed dead	12/ 7/15
708	Pte.	Thomson, C., Hawick, Rox.	Missing, presumed dead	12/ 7/15
6744	Pte.	Taylor, W., Galashiels, Sel.	Missing, presumed dead	12/ 7/15
6380	L./Sgt.	Waddell, A., Galashiels, Sel.	Missing, presumed dead	12/ 7/15
6737	Pte.	Walls, W., Tillicoultry, Cla.	Missing, presumed dead	12/ 7/15
6867	Pte.	Whitelaw, D., Symington, Lan.	Missing, presumed dead	12/ 7/15
6881	L./Cpl.	Waldie, W., Cavers, Rox.	Missing, presumed dead	12/ 7/15
6125	Sgt.	Whyte, J., Melrose, Rox.	Died of wounds	12/ 7/15
6645	Pte.	Walker, W., Motherwell, Lan.	Killed in action	12/ 7/15

6613	Pte.	Walker, W., Portsmouth, Hants.	Killed in action	12/ 7/15
4545	Pte.	Webb, W., Melrose, Rox.	Killed in action	12/ 7/15
811	Pte.	Wilson, A., Peebles, Peeb.	Killed in action	12/ 7/15
6916	Pte.	Weatherston, J., Galashiels, Sel.	Killed in action	12/ 7/15
7112	Pte.	Watson, R., Earlston, Ber.	Killed in action	12/ 7/15
7246	Pte.	Wright, J., St. Boswells, Rox.	Killed in action	12/ 7/15
480	Sgt.	Walker, J., Wilton, Rox.	Killed in action	12/ 7/15
7304	Pte.	Waters, J., Kelso, Rox.	Missing, presumed dead	12/ 7/15
7247	Pte.	Wishart, T., Crieff, Per.	Missing, presumed dead	12/ 7/15
4387	Pte.	Watt, C., Berwick-upon-Tweed, Nor.	Missing, presumed dead	12/ 7/15
830	Pte.	Wight, T., Hawick, Rox.	Missing, presumed dead	12/ 7/15
4436	Pte.	White, J., Lauder, Ber.	Missing, presumed dead	12/ 7/15
4203	Pte.	Wilson, R., Coldingham, Ber.	Missing, presumed dead	12/ 7/15
922	Pte.	Whillans, R., Hawick, Rox.	Missing, presumed dead	12/ 7/15
546	Pte.	Wallace, B., Kelso, Rox.	Missing, presumed dead	12/ 7/15
4032	C.S.M.	Wood, J., Duns, Ber.	Missing, presumed dead	12/ 7/15
6475	Pte.	Wood, K., Galashiels, Sel.	Missing, presumed dead	12/ 7/15
6452	C.S.M.	Watson, D., Fettercairn, Kin.	Missing, presumed dead	12/ 7/15
7432	Pte.	Wilson, J., Carham, Nor.	Missing, presumed dead	12/ 7/15
566	Pte.	Wait, J., Southdean, Hawick	Missing, presumed dead	12/ 7/15
492	Pte.	Whittaker, T., Wilton, Rox.	Missing, presumed dead	12/ 7/15
557	Pte.	Waldie, J., Hawick, Rox.	Missing, presumed dead	12/ 7/15
4499	Pte.	Waddell, R., Duns, Ber.	Missing, presumed dead	12/ 7/15
6464	A./Sgt.	Waite, J., Yarrow, Sel.	Missing, presumed dead	12/ 7/15
6558	Pte.	Weir, R., Galashiels, Sel.	Missing, presumed dead	12/ 7/15
6668	Cpl.	Yule, C., Galashiels, Sel.	Missing, presumed dead	12/ 7/15
7090	Pte.	Young, G., Galashiels, Sel.	Missing, presumed dead	12/ 7/15
6920	Pte.	Young, R., Earlston, Ber.	Missing, presumed dead	12/ 7/15
7189	Pte.	Yeomans, R., Kelso, Rox.	Missing, presumed dead	12/ 7/15
7448	Pte.	Aitken, J., Moffat, Dum.	Died of wounds	19/ 7/15
7655	Pte.	Bennett, T., Galashiels, Sel.	Died of wounds	13/ 7/15
7249	Pte.	Brunton, J., Galashiels, Sel.	Died of wounds	17/ 7/15
7394	Pte.	Brodie, C., Selkirk, Sel.	Died of wounds	19/ 7/15
825	Pte.	Brannan, A., Hawick, Rox.	Died of disease	9/12/15
4408	Pte.	Crow, R., Kelso, Rox.	Died of disease	17/10/15
6433	Bugler	Currie, W., Galashiels, Sel.	Died of disease	29/10/15
6591	Pte.	Donaldson, W., Galashiels, Sel.	Died of wounds	17/ 7/15
7150	Pte.	Dumma, R., Roxburgh, Rox.	Died of disease	4/11/15
6550	L./Cpl.	Dick, D., Edinburgh, Mid.	Died of disease	10/11/15
777	Pte.	Edmunds, R., Edinburgh, Mid.	Died of wounds	20/ 7/15
555	Pte.	Fortune, J., Ednam, Rox.	Died of disease	20/10/15
871	Pte.	Gray, A., Hawick, Rox.	Died of disease	27/10/15
4398	L./Cpl.	Hume, R., Ayton, Ber.	Died of wounds	25/ 7/15
7739	Pte.	Holywell, H., Duns, Ber.	Died of disease	8/ 8/15
586	Pte.	Hope, D., Jedburgh, Rox.	Died of wounds	21/ 7/15
7627	Pte.	Jackson, G., Lilliesleaf, Rox.	Died of disease	29/ 7/15
7460	Pte.	Kyle, J., Hawick, Rox.	Died of wounds	14/ 7/15
7076	Pte.	Kerr, J., Earlston, Ber.	Died of disease	19/10/15
6850	L./Cpl.	Kerr, F., Ancrum, Rox.	Died of wounds	20/10/15

778	Pte.	Lunham, T., Nenthorn, Rox.	Died of wounds	24/ 7/15
7229	Pte.	Middlemas, J., Eccles, Ber	Killed in action	4/ 9/15
6780	Pte.	Matthews, W., Haddingtonshire	Killed in action	11/10/15
7631	Pte.	Martin, A., Dublin, Dub.	Killed accidentally	21/11/15
7397	Pte.	Nichol, T., Carlisle, Cum.	Died of wounds	17/12/15
7168	Pte.	Purves, T., Duns, Ber	Died of wounds	14/ 7/15
658	Pte.	Riddell, A., Hawick, Rox.	Died of wounds	13/ 7/15
6742	Pte.	Redpath, A., Hawick, Rox.	Killed accidentally	5/ 9/15
7429	Pte.	Reid, R., Hawick, Rox.	Died of wounds	30/ 7/15
6761	Pte.	Shiels, W., Galashiels, Sel.	Died of disease	13/ 7/15
7376	Pte.	Swan, A., Reston, Ber	Died of wounds	13/ 7/15
7475	Pte.	Smith, J., Hawick, Rox.	Died of wounds	13/ 7/15
4396	Pte.	Smerdon, C., London, Midx.	Died of wounds	14/ 7/15
6474	Pte.	Smail, A., Galashiels, Sel.	Died of disease	25/11/15
6765	Pte.	Turnbull, W., Earlston, Ber	Died of wounds	15/ 7/15
662	Pte.	Turnbull, R., Hawick, Rox.	Died of disease	9/ 9/15
4501	Pte.	Wilson, J., Hawick, Rox.	Died of wounds	13/ 7/15
4127	Sgt.	Wilson, J., Hawick, Rox.	Died of wounds	15/ 7/15
6833	Pte.	Wright, J., Kelso, Rox.	Died of wounds	26/ 7/15
6726	Pte.	Wallis, W., Morley, York.	Died of wounds	18/12/15
753	Pte.	Wright, A., Kelso, Rox.	Died of wounds	20/10/15
4435	Pte.	White, G., Lauder, Ber	Died of disease	27/11/15
729	L./Cpl.	Wood, F., Newton Don, Rox.	Died of disease	4/12/15

Kings Own Scottish Borderers attacking the Turks at Gallipoli in 1915. (IWM).

The Year 1916 – Northern France and the Battle of the Somme

At the start of 1916, the war was not going well for Britain and the Allies. The regular and volunteer armies had been so seriously depleted that there was an urgent need for more men. Although over 1 million men had volunteered since 1914, it was still not enough and on 9th February 1916 conscription began for men aged between 18 and 41. During the course of the war, over 4.5 million Britons served in the armed forces with a further 3 million from across the British Empire. Countries that sent the most soldiers included Canada, India, South Africa, Australia and New Zealand.

During the early winter of 1915, competitive Rugby League games ceased at Oldham. Charlie was released from his contract and returned to Kelso. On 24th February 1916 he took up his post in the British Army. Charlie had been a volunteer soldier before the war. He left Kelso and boarded the train to North Wales, to join the Royal Engineers at their training camp in Deganwy. He underwent eight weeks of basic but intense training, before departing for France. It would be 3 long years before he would return to Kelso again, to settle down to family life. Charlie was 28 years old, a professional Rugby League player and in peak physical condition. The next 3 years took a heavy toll on his body.

The British Empire in WW1

The British Empire during 1914-18; the largest empire the world had ever known. It held sway over 20% of the world's population (www.ozed.com).

Summary of spring and early summer 1916

'By the Spring of 1916, Germany's response to the stagnating situation on the Western Front was to undertake a huge offensive at Verdun in February. The Germans hoped to defeat the French Army in one decisive blow. Between February and December 1916, the French and German armies incurred over one million casualties. In an attempt to relieve the pressure on the French at Verdun, the British and French undertook a push to the north at the Somme, and on the first day of the battle (1st July 1916), 20,000 Britons were killed and a further 40,000 injured. Tanks were used for the first time in war (on the Somme in July) but they were to have very limited effect, due to their heavy weight, slow speed and cumbersome nature. They didn't cope well with the mud or the bomb-cratered terrain of the battlefields. British tanks did have a psychological effect on the Germans, as Germany had very few of her own.

On the oceans, both the British and German navies continued to engage in battles to determine control of the shipping channels. At the battle of Jutland, in the North Sea, on 31st of May 1916, the British Grand Fleet under Admiral Jellicoe engaged the German navy and caused significant damage. The British lost more ships and men in the battle but the German fleet was more heavily affected. The German navy spent most of the rest of the war in its home ports. This allowed the British fleet to take control of the seas, allowing troops, military supplies and food to reach the battlefields of Europe with much greater frequency.

As the war continued, changes took place which affected the lives of people back home in Britain. The British government was running out of money and in February, a scheme for National Savings was introduced to increase government access to funds. On the 21st of May, a measure to ensure daylight saving (British summertime) was introduced to allow for greater production or war materials in the factories. There were still problems to be dealt with on the home front. Ireland had been on poor terms with Britain for many generations. A proportion of the Irish population wished for independence from the United Kingdom. On the 24th of April 1916, with British attention focussed on the Western Front, an armed uprising (the Easter Rising) took place in Dublin, in an attempt to gain Irish independence. Michael Collins was one of the key 'Irish Rebels'. The rebels gained support from Germany and were supplied with guns and ammunition. An Irish Republic was proclaimed but the rising was soon crushed by the British Government. Many of the rebel leaders were executed. An Irish Republic was eventually created in 1922.'

(Source - BBC History)

Charles Robeson's involvement in the First World War

Charlie Robeson enlisted as a sapper in the Royal Engineers, part of Lord Kitchener's Army on 24th February 1916 and was mobilised on 24th April 1916.

Charlie (Ypres, December 1917), in the uniform of the 225th Field Company Royal Engineers (39th Division), which was part of General Gough's 5th Army in France. The 225th Field Company was affiliated with the town of Stockton-on-Tees. Along with the 227th and 234th (Stockton) Field Companies, the entire 39th Division's contribution has been largely overlooked, in the history of the Great War. They played a hugely significant role in at least 13 major battlefield engagements, including four battles at the Somme in 1916, five battles at Passchendaele in 1917 and four battles at the Somme, in the German Spring Offensive of 1918.

Basic training for the Royal Engineers in North Wales, before leaving for France

Conway training camp, which was used by the Royal Engineers in WWI, (Authors collection)
was located across the estuary from Deganwy (Photographed in 1911).

Deganwy training camp (in foreground) with Conway Camp (in background). This is where (Authors collection)
Charlie and his intake of Royal Engineers were sent for training in the spring of 1916.

A postcard from Charlie at his training camp in North Wales

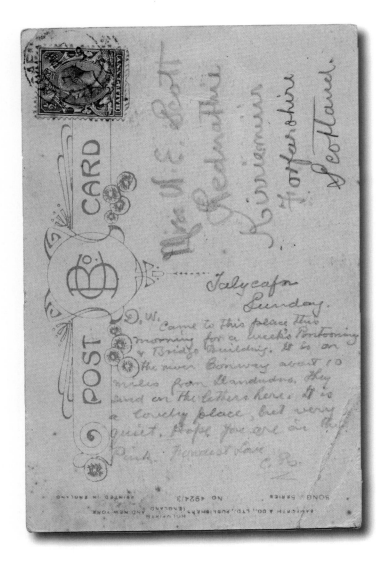

Posted by Charlie in May 1916 –
It reads:

Talycafn, Sunday.

Dear Winnie, (D.W.)
'Came to this place this morning for a weeks pontooning and bridge building. It is on the River Conway about 10 miles from Llandudno. They send on the letters here. It is a lovely place but very quiet. Hope you are in the pink.'
Fondest Love, Charlie (C.R.).

In return, a postcard from Kelso, sent to Charlie in Wales during this time.

(Authors collection)

Spring 1916, with No 5 Company Royal Engineers on parade at their training ground at Deganwy in North Wales. Charlie is 4th from right in front row. One of Charlie's friends, Fred Haines, is 1st in the second row. (Later in the war, Fred was killed on the eve of his return home. He was due to be married to Charlie's fiancées sister, Flo).

Charlie back row extreme left – at training in North Wales in the Spring 1916 before leaving for France.

Charlie at the age of 28, displaying a keen spirit with rifle, bayonet and field pack in the Spring of 1916, North Wales Training Camp.

Arrival in France

After initial training, Charlie sailed across the Channel and landed in France, at the port of Le Havre (29th July 1916), at the mouth of the River Seine.

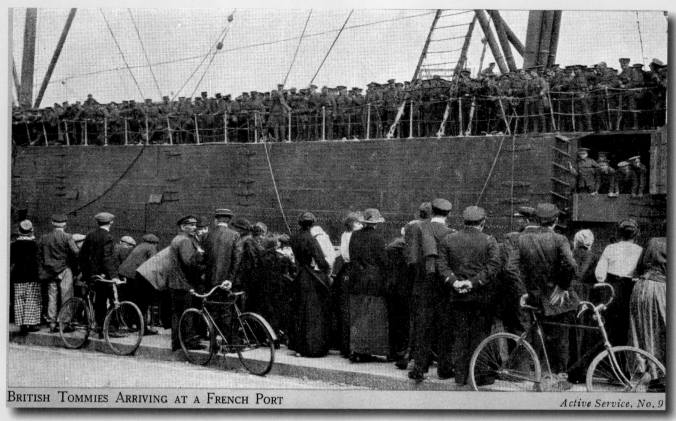

BRITISH TOMMIES ARRIVING AT A FRENCH PORT

Active Service, No. 9

British 'Tommies' arriving by ship at a French port (possibly Le Havre).

(Authors collection)

Postcard sent by Charlie from Rouen (a main British Army staging camp), whilst travelling by boat up the River Seine from Le Havre, en route to the Front.

338 ROUEN   Vue Générale des Quais et Bon-Secours   General view of the Quays and Bon-Secours

(Authors collection)

Charlie writes to Winnie from Rouen: 'Just a card to thank you for the postcard sent me. Hope you had a good holiday. Well, we landed here on Monday after a very pleasant sail across the Channel & up the river- The scenery was splendid. Rouen is a very pretty place. We are having very warm weather.' (Posted from No 5 Cavalry Detail Auxiliary Camp, Rouen, France. Post marked 29th July 1916. Passed by Field Censor 1476.)

Royal Engineers cap badge in WWI with King George V insignia.

Charlie was recruited into the Royal Engineers rather than his local infantry regiment, The Kings Own Scottish Borderers

Charlie had a keen analytical mind but was also very practical and was used to handling tools. It was his experience with horses (he had trained and worked as a saddler and harness maker) that made him attractive to the Royal Engineers. The Engineers depended on horses for transporting the many tons of equipment needed at the Front every day. Men like Charlie could repair horse harnesses and leatherwork. Charlie was also an excellent shot. He competed in shooting competitions at Bisley, before the war. Charlie was trained as a Sapper by the Engineers. A Sapper was an Engineer Soldier whose principal job was to dig tunnels and lay explosives under enemy lines. Much of the time, the Engineers dug trenches. Engineers were armed with rifles and bayonets and fought alongside Frontline troops.

The role of the Royal Engineers (RE)

A Group of Royal Engineers on a bridge that they have constructed over the Somme. Royal Engineers wore soft flat caps (rather than tin helmets) most of the time. (NLS).

'Although not an Infantry Battalion, the Royal Engineers (RE) carried rifles and accompanied (and fought alongside) all front line infantry battalions in WWI. The Royal Engineers supplied the front line troops with all their equipment and built and maintained the railways, roads, water supplies, bridges and transport. They laid communication wires and maintained the telephones, wireless and other signalling equipment. They dug the trenches, built artillery positions and all front-line fortifications. Without the Royal Engineers, the infantry and artillery would have been powerless, as they also maintained the guns and other weapons.'

(Source - The Long Long Trail).

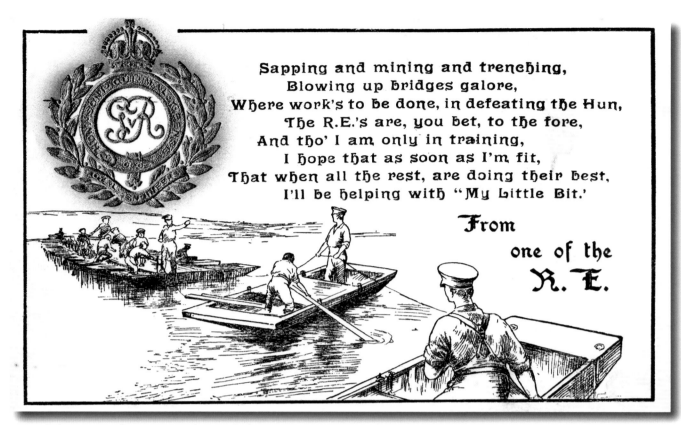

Sapping and mining and trenching,
Blowing up bridges galore,
Where work's to be done, in defeating the Hun,
The R.E.'s are, you bet, to the fore,
And tho' I am only in training,
I hope that as soon as I'm fit,
That when all the rest, are doing their best,
I'll be helping with "My Little Bit."

From one of the R.E.

Postcard showing Royal Engineers working on bridging pontoons.

(Authors collection)

The number of Royal Engineers required during the war

Before August 1914, the Royal Engineers had consisted of approximately 1,000 officers and 10,000 men of the regular army. By November, the Royal Engineers had grown to around 17,000 officers and 340,000 other ranks.

Charlie belonged to the 225th Field Company, 39th Division, Royal Engineers.

A Field Company was composed of 217 men, which was made up of the following:

- A Major, who was in command of the Company.
- A Captain, who was second in command.
- 3 Lieutenants (or Second Lieutenants), one each commanding a Section.
- 23 Non Commissioned Officers (Company Sergeant-Major, Company Quartermaster Sergeant, Farrier Sergeant, 6 Sergeants, 7 Corporals, and seven 2nd-Corporals (a rank peculiar to the Royal Engineers and Army Ordnance Corps).
- 186 other ranks (1 Shoeing Smith, 1 Trumpeter, 1 Bugler, 138 Sappers, 37 Drivers, 8 Batmen).
- 2 attached Privates of the Royal Army Medical Corps for water duties.
- 1 attached Driver of the Army Service Corps.

(Source – The Long Long Trail)

Charlie Robeson was a sapper. A sapper was a tunneler. The word derives from earlier battles, when tunnels were dug under enemy fortifications to 'sap' their strength. Royal Engineer sappers were expert at laying explosives under enemy trenches. Charlie spent most of his time digging and repairing frontline trenches with the Engineers and fighting alongside the Infantry.

'The men chosen to join the conscripted Royal Engineers were selected on the skills and trades they had in civilian life. Trades required by the army in the field included; farriers, blacksmiths, bricklayers, builders, engineers, tool operators, stockmen, carpenters, clerks, stone masons, painters, plumbers, surveyors, draughtsmen, wheelwrights, engine drivers, saddlers, harness makers and many others.

The Field Companies relied on horses for transport and each Company had 17 riding horses for the officers and non commissioned officers, plus 50 draught heavy horses and 4 pack horses. With the exceptions of the Trumpeter and Bugler, all other ranks were armed as infantrymen and carried rifles. Each Company had in its care approximately 110 shovels and 105 pickaxes. It also carried a store of sandbags and guncotton charges.'

(Source – The Long Long Trail)

Royal Engineers attending the Horse Lines at their training ground at Aldershot, before the war.   (Authors collection)

Royal Engineers moving men and equipment behind the lines at night. During the war, movement of men and equipment took place in the dark, to avoid detection. (Authors collection)

A Royal Engineers Field Company

What a Royal Engineers Field Company looked like in the Field. (Authors collection)

A Royal Engineers Field Company moving pontoon bridging materials. (Authors collection)

Where Charlie and the 39th Division fought during the war

The 225th Field Company Royal Engineers was part of the 39th Division, which began forming in August 1915. It was sent to France in March 1916. It suffered heavy losses on the Somme in 1916, catastrophic losses at Passchendaele in 1917 and was virtually wiped out on the Somme (again) during the German offensive in 1918. The Division was disbanded in the summer of 1919.

The 39th Division consisted of the following units:

116th Brigade	11th, 12th, 13th and 14th Royal Sussex Regiments and 14th Hampshire Regiment.
117th Brigade	16th and 17th Sherwood Foresters,17th Kings Royal Rifle Company and 16th Rifle Brigade.
118th Brigade	1/6th Cheshire Regiment,1/1st Cambridgeshire Regiment, 1/1st Herts Regiment and the 4th/5th Black Watch Regiment.
Pioneers	13th Gloucestershire Regiment.
Royal Engineers	225th, 227th and 234th Field Companies.
South Irish Horse	E Company.
Royal Field Artillery	V.39 Heavy Mortar Battery.
Machine Gun Company	228th and 39th Battalion Company.
Royal Army Medical Corps	132nd, 133rd and 134th Field Ambulance.

All the battles described in this book are battles in which Charlie fought.

1916 – The Somme (Northern France)

An attack near Richebourg L'Avoue (30th June) in which the Sussex Battalions suffered heavy casualties.

- The Fighting on the Ancre.★
- The Battle of Thiepval Ridge.★
- The Battle of the Ancre Heights★ including the capture of the Schwaben Redoubt and Stuff Trench.
- The Battle of the Ancre.★

  (The battles marked ★ are phases of the Battles of the Somme 1916)

> 'The 39th Division was mobilised in March 1916 and embarked immediately for France. The Division crossed the Channel and arrived at the port of Le Havre. All units were concentrated near Blaringhem and moved quickly to the Somme. The Division remained on the Western Front for the duration of the war.'
>
> (Source – The Long Long Trail)

1917 – Passchendaele (Ypres, Belgium)

- The Battle of Pilckem Ridge.★★
- The Battle of Langemarck.★★
- The Battle of the Menin Road Ridge.★★
- The Battle of Polygon Wood.★★
- The Second Battle of Passchendaele.★★

  (The battles marked ★★ are phases of the Third Battles of Ypres 1917) better known as Passchendaele

1918 – The Somme

- The Battle of St Quentin.★★★
- The actions at the Somme Crossings.★★★
- The Battle of Bapaume.★★★
- The Battle of Rosieres.★★★

  (The battles marked ★★★ are phases of the First Battles of the Somme 1918)

1918 – Flanders

- The fighting on Wytschaete Ridge.++
- The First Battle of Kemmel.++
- The Second Battle of Kemmel.++
- The Battle of the Scherpenberg.++

  (The battles marked ++ are phases of the Battles of the Lys)

NB: A full Division consisted of between 10,000 and 15,000 men. This means that the entire 39th Division was replaced by new recruits at least twice between 1914 and 1918. Charlie was very fortunate to survive the war.

'After suffering heavy losses during the Battles of the Lys, a decision was taken to reduce the Division down to a Cadre (a small unit of specially trained soldiers). This took place by 1st June 1918. After this it was engaged in supervising courses of instruction for American troops, beginning with units of the 77th American Division.

Divisional HQ was based at Eperlecques from 11th April to 7th June 1918; it then went to Wolphus and then Varengueville (from 15th August) and finally to Rouen (5th March 1919).

The Division was reconstituted, by taking over the 197th Brigade (ex 66th Division) and the Brigade at the malarial camp at St Martin Eglise. These units operated embarkation camps and reinforcement depots in early 1919. Demobilisation continued and by 10th July 1919, the Division ceased to exist.

The Great War cost 39th Division 27,869 men killed, wounded or missing.'

(Source – The Long Long Trail)

Charlie's first real experience of war, at the Battle of the Somme in 1916

'The main focus for British activity in France during 1916 was in the valley of the River Somme. Mile upon mile of trenches had been dug in the chalk white soils in the spring, in preparation for a major offensive in the summer. The British chose to focus attention on a small area of ground extending along a short front of only 20 miles. The most intense fighting took place between Albert, Bapaume and Peronne over a 5 month period from July to November. The week before battle commenced on 1st July, a seven day artillery barrage by the British, fired over 1,700,000 shells into enemy held territory. It was intended to crush the German defences. It didn't.

The Somme was the first major battle of 1916, in which the Conscripted Army took the leading role. It was supposed to have been a joint venture with the French but the French were exhausted after battles at Verdun. It was also unusual in that the army was drawn from all levels of society in Britain and from all countries of the British Empire. The men had been encouraged to join up en masse and been incorporated into battalions of men who knew each other well; 'the Pals Battalions'. This system of recruitment was to prove devastating, as whole generations of young men were wiped out leaving local communities back home psychologically traumatised and physically handicapped.

Battlefield technology included increasingly sophisticated trench systems with a complex network of underground tunnels. These were dug and used by Royal Engineer sappers to lay mines, with the aim of blowing up enemy trenches. Large and extensive concrete shelters and emplacements were constructed (more so by the Germans). In 1916, for the first time, aeroplanes were used for reconnaissance and to drop bombs'.

(Source – BBC History)

On arrival at the Somme in July, Charlie joined the 39th Division and was immediately posted to the battlefield Frontline between Beaumont Hamel and Thiepval. This area was to become one of the fiercest battle grounds on the Somme during the summer and autumn of 1916. Over the succeeding five months, the 39th Division was to fight constantly across and along short sections of the British Frontline, to the north east of the town of Albert.

Battlefield map of the Somme

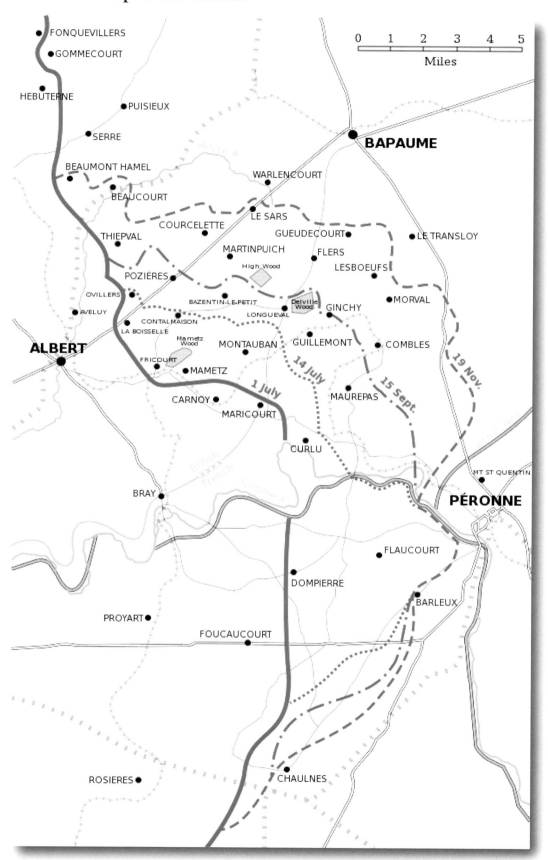

Map showing the Battle of the Somme, July-November 1916. The concentration of British activity was fought across a relatively small but incredibly intensive battle front, only 20 miles across. Charlie spent the summer and autumn of 1916 fighting between Beaumont Hamel and Thiepval. The red lines show the slow pace of the British advance. (www.epsomandewellhistoryexplorer.org)

The following is a summary of the major engagements involving Charlie's Company, the 225th Field Company Royal Engineers (39th Division) throughout the second half of 1916. It gives a quick overview of what the fighting was like.

The Battle of the Somme- 1st July to 18th November 1916 (Source - The Long Long Trail)

The opening phase 1st – 13th July

The first day of the battle is recorded as being the bloodiest day in the history of the British Army, with over 60,000 casualties recorded.

'The British assault broke into and gradually moved beyond the first of the German defensive complexes on the Somme. Success on the first day in the area between Montauban and Mametz, led to a redirection of effort to that area, for the initial attack had been defeated, with huge losses incurred north of Mametz. There was a stiff fight for Trones Wood and costly, hastily planned and piecemeal attacks that eventually took La Boisselle, Contalmaison and Mametz Wood.'

By the 13th of July

'The British advance had taken it to a point where it was now facing the second German defensive complex. A well planned night attack on 14th July took British troops through that line but they now ran into stiffening enemy defence at Guillemont, Delville Wood and Longueval, High Wood and Pozieres. Attack and counter-attack ground relentlessly on as the British edged forward.'

'A renewal of the offensive finally broke through the area that had proved to be so difficult since 14th July. Using a small number of tanks for the first time in history, the British Army finally captured High Wood and pressed on through Flers and up the Bapaume road to Courcelette.'

By 23rd September

'Having broken through the prepared lines of German defence, the British now faced a new set of challenges as it approached the slopes of the Transloy ridges. Fighting was, as before, severe but gradually the British chipped away and pushed forward. The weather began to deteriorate, bringing heavy rain, making the battlefield increasingly difficult and stretching men to limits of their physical endurance.'

The Battle of Thiepval Ridge 26th – 28th September 1916

Charlie and the 39th Division to this point, had mostly been in Reserve positions supporting the infantry at Thiepval. The Division then became heavily involved in the following engagements at the Front Line.

The Battle of the Ancre Heights, 1st October – 11th November 1916

'As a necessary preliminary to the Reserve Army's part in General Haig's projected large scale autumn offensive, General Gough sought to secure the whole of Thiepval Ridge. This necessitated the capture, in full, of those intricate defensive positions which had repeatedly blocked the way to the vital high ground during the September fighting: the Schwaben Redoubt, Stuff Redoubt and Regina Trench. Between 1st and 8th October the Canadian Corps assaults on Regina Trench witnessed brutal fighting, heavy casualties and temporary limited occupation of the objective. Meanwhile, in a confusing succession of attacks, the 18th and 39th Divisions struggled unremittingly to clear the Schwaben Redoubt of its last defenders. Stuff Redoubt was stormed just after midday on 9th October and following vicious actions, the Schwaben Redoubt finally succumbed to the 39th Division in the afternoon of 14th October. The weather and appalling battlefield conditions delayed further operations; it was not until 21st October that renewed efforts against Regina trench (and the adjoining Stuff trench) were possible. Two Corps infantry attacked on a 5,000 yard front at 12.06pm, well supported by artillery and after sharp fighting took all their objectives, in just over 30 minutes. The whole of the crest of the ridge was now in British hands. Canadian attempts on 23rd October further to extend their occupation of Regina Trench, were frustrated by mud and heavy enemy fire. It was not until 10th November, after days of rain, that a surprise midnight assault finally secured the eastern portion of this position.

Thiepval Ridge had been one of the strong points in the German first line that had proved so impossible for the British attack on 1st July. Now outflanked to the east, Thiepval and the heights on which it sat, fell to an efficiently executed attack. Left alone since the failure of 1st July, the slopes of the area on either side of the River Ancre were attacked time and again in wet, foggy and wintry conditions, with Beaumont Hamel finally falling into British hands in mid November.'

(Source – www.gwgc.org)

The end of 1916 and the Battle of the Somme

By late November 1916, the Germans had suffered very serious loss of life and territorial ground. The German Command made a decision to withdraw to the pre-determined and heavily fortified Hindenburg Line, many miles to the east. The 39th Division had played a hugely significant part in the Battle of the Somme.

The WWI War Diaries of the 225th Field Company (39th Division) Royal Engineers

War Diaries were kept by each Company Commander, for the duration of the war. The War Diaries for the 225th Field Company Royal Engineers list in detail the day to day movements of Charlie's Company, so we can track where he was and what he was doing, on an almost daily basis. The Diaries cover from March 1915, when the Company was formed, to March 1919, when it was disbanded. Many War Diaries were destroyed in WW2.

A War Diary was a daily record of operations, intelligence reports and other events, kept for each Company by an appointed junior officer. They were not personal accounts but official documents. Many of them were scribbled hastily in pencil and they used obscure abbreviations, which can be difficult to read. Surviving copies of British Army War Diaries are kept at the National Archives in London.

The following information was extracted from the official War Diaries of the 225th Field Company Royal Engineers, retained at the National Archives. It follows the day to day movements of the Company (and therefore of Sapper Charlie Robeson) from Thiepval on the Somme (1916) to Canal Bank at Ypres & Passchendaele (1917) and back across the Western Front to the Somme at St. Quentin (1918). The War Diary entries are by their nature more descriptive than narrative.

For most of the war, entries in the Diaries were written by Major D. H. Hammonds, Officer Commanding, 225th Field Company, Royal Engineers. Major Hammonds was killed on March 30th 1918. (On this date, Charlie Robeson won the Military Medal 'For Bravery in the Field,' for eliminating the German sniper who killed his Company Commander; Major Hammonds).

In the following War Diary extracts of the 225th Field Company RE, place names and trench names were written in capital letters for clarity. The words are copied verbatim from the actual Diaries (Courtesy National Archives).

Place	Date	WAR DIARY or INTELLIGENCE SUMMARY	Signed by

Summary of information of the 225th Field Company, 39th Division, Royal Engineers

The Formation of the 225th Field Company RE

Place	Date		Signed by
Stockton	May 1915	In the early spring of 1915, the Mayor of STOCKTON Alderman Stephenson was empowered by the war office to train a company of Royal Engineers (RE)….. The 225th Field Company.	
		Recruiting commenced on 20th May and was completed by 3rd June. Recruiting carried on to complete a further 2 Companies, the 227th and 234th.	
		At first, there were no training facilities but by 1st June MARTON HALL near STOCKTON was taken over and formal training started. Much assistance was received from the local neighbourhood in supplying materials for field work. Instructors were sent from Chatham in Kent, to take charge of training.	
		The formation of the 3 Companies named above, was put under the immediate charge of N. S. A Harrison, a local gentleman, who was given the rank of Major. He soon appointed as sub alterns; Messer's Argent, Heavisides, Scott and Wilkinson and later Mr Paton as reserve officer. These officers were away in turn, attending courses of pontooning at FISKERTON and field works at NEWARK training centres.	
Aldershot	Oct 1915	On Oct 8th the Company moved to ALDERSHOT, where it was issued with wagons but still had no rifles or equipment.	
Milford Surrey		On 10th October, the company moved to MILFORD CAMP and joined the 39th Division to complete its training. Rifles and equipment were issued and full mobilisation stores completed. Some combined training was carried out with special attention paid to trench work.	
	Nov 1915	Capt D. H. Hammonds (RE) joined the Company on 25th November from the 54th Company (7th Division), after 9 months experience in France.	
	Jan 1916	On 20th January 1916, the Company returned to ALDERSHOT and completed its musketry training at CAESAR'S CAMP ranges, relieving to MILFORD CAMP on completion. Throughout November, December, January and February, the training was much impeded by exceptionally wet weather.	
		The supply of materials for field works at MILFORD was very limited and it was not until February that sufficient barbed wire could be obtained to train the men in this essential detail.	

	Feb 1916	On Feb 24th the Division was to have been reviewed by the King but this was put off owing to heavy snow.	
		The Company was finally warned to entrain for overseas on March 1st and after two postponements of 24hrs, left MILFORD CAMP on March 3rd 1916.	
		D.H. Hammonds Capt RE	

Crossing over to France

Milford Surrey	3/3/16	Entrained at GODALMING for SOUTHAMPTON. Crossed on ship called 'City of Benares' leaving at 4.30pm.	DHH Capt RE
Le Havre	4/3/16	Disembarked at LE HAVRE. Marched to rest camp for the night.	
	5/3/16	Entrained at MARCHANDISE station.	
Steenbecque	6/3/16	Detrained at STEENBECQUE station and marched to billets near the station.	
	7-8/3/16	In billets at STEENBECQUE. Major N. S. A Harrison became sick with pleurisy and sent to the 2nd Canadian clearing station at AIRE.	
Nouveau Monde	9/3/16	Marched to billets at NOUVEAU near ESTAIRES.	

Arrival at the Front (on the Somme)

Somme (near Bethune)	10/3/16	The Company being attached to the 8th Division for training was put under the orders of Major Betty RE, Officer Commanding (OC) 15th Field Company (Fld Coy). Lt Lambert of that Company was attached as instructor. A portion of the 8th Division was allotted to the Company. 'D' Company of the 13th GLOUCESTERS (Pioneers of the 39th Division) was attached to work under the Company. The portion of the FRONT allotted, was from ROTTEN ROW trench to BOND STREET trench inclusive.	DHH Capt RE
Nouveau Monde	11-14/3/16	Work consisted mainly in making a reserve line of trenches about 400 yards from the FRONT LINE and by retrieving the communication trenches by putting down pathways of trench gratings and revetting the sides.	
		The system of work was to subdivide the FRONT between the 4 Sections of REs and to give each a platoon of the Pioneer Company at its disposal. The men were sent up as near to the work as possible in wagons each day. 7hrs work in trenches by day and 5hrs work by night was insisted upon.	DHH Capt RE
Somme (north of Arras)	15/3/16	Rest day. This was in accord with the 8th Divisions system of giving a rest day every 8th day when possible, coinciding with a night of relief in the trenches. On these days, wagons were cleaned and overhauled, rifles and equipment were inspected.	
	16-22/3/16	Work carried on as above. Infantry parties were employed on an average of 200 by day and 150 by night. These were distributed to the sections as required.	DHH

British troops moving along a communication trench. (NLS)

A wiring party going over a shell-swept area. (NLS)

	24/3/16	Orders were received to march to Rest Area on 25th March. The day was spent collecting tools for handing over and packing wagons.	DHH
Lacouture	26/3/16	The day was spent going round new trenches with guides from 81st Company RE. We visited General Officer Commanding (GOC) 58th Brigade (BDE) and arranged work to be undertaken. The situation was that 19th Division had taken over the whole FRONT of the 35th Division. Hence, extra Field Companies were required to assist. The FRONT was from QUINQUE RUE trench to PLUM STREET trench.	
Somme (between Bethune & Arras)	27/3/16	Work started on FRONT LINE parapet at ROPE communication trench. Owing to collapse of the trenches during the winter, the right section was in very bad condition. Two gaps in the front parapet existed through which communication was impossible by day. ROPE trench was the only communication trench existing to the right section and no complete support on the reserve line existed. Hence, work was of a very important nature. Only 200 infantry were allowed per night. Weather very bad. Heavy rain and wind.	DHH

Silk Postcards

Charlie communicated constantly with Winnie by post. Soldiers got mail delivered to the Frontline every day.
Many silk postcards such as this one were sent by my grandfather to my grandmother in 1916.

Letters to and from home were written in their thousands

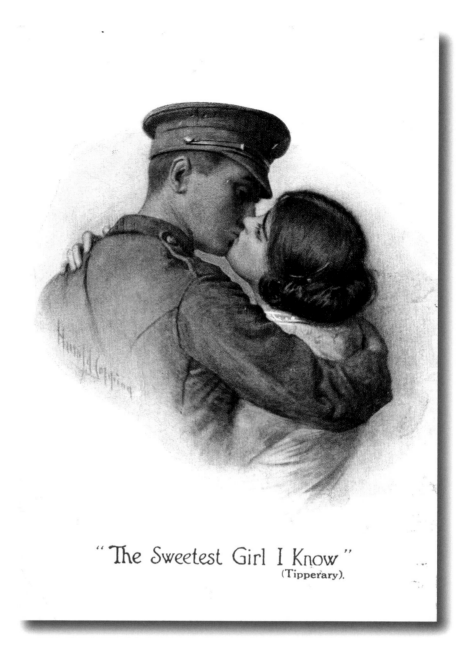

"The Sweetest Girl I Know"
(Tipperary).

Charlie was a long way from home.

Personal letters and cards were eagerly awaited by soldiers and their families. Most correspondence was censored (read) by officers so as not to give vital information to the enemy, should the letters be intercepted by the Germans.

Pictures of Home

The north side of Kelso Bridge, Roxburghshire.   (Authors collection)

Kelso Square and Town Hall.   (Authors collection)

Lacouture	28/3/16	Work taken over on 4 observation posts on RUE De BOIS trench. These were to consist of brick chimneys built inside ruined houses. Also several Machine Gun emplacements and strong dug-outs and repairs to tramways were undertaken. Supplies of stores were taken to 2 Battalions of Infantry in FRONT LINE. Weather still bad.	DHH Capt RE
	31/3/16	Three sections had their rest day. Major N. S. A Harrison rejoined the Company.	DHH
Somme (between Bethune & Arras)	1/4/16	New work started on clearing CADBURY trench. A complete machine gun emplacement was put in near BOARS HEAD. A pack horse died of pneumonia.	Major NSA Harrison
	3/4/16	Work continued. One sapper was wounded today.	NSAH
	4/4/16	A new machine gun emplacement was put in at COPSE KEEP. Also screening of RUE DE BOIS trench with willow stakes was undertaken.	
	5/4/16	The Company took over control of GRUB STREET tramway.	NSAH
	8/4/16	Rest day on account of infantry relief. Day spent cleaning billets and wagons etc.	NSAH
	12-14/4/16	General fatigue. Preparing to evacuate to LE TOURET to join the 39th Division. Captain Hammonds evacuated to hospital.	
Le Touret	16/4/16	Company removed to LE TOURET.	
Somme (near Bethune)	19/4/16	Sgt Midgeley wounded. One driver and one sapper evacuated to hospital and one sapper arrived as reinforcement. Work commenced on PIONEER, SHETLAND, FIFE and BARNTON communication trenches. Company worked on observation post at CORNER HOUSE and ADVANCED TELEPHONE STATION.	
	20-21/4/16	Continued work on above and also at Batteries A174 and B174. Worked on gun pits, tramways, machine gun emplacements in FIFE trench and dressing station at FESTUBERT CENTRAL.	NSAH

A party of British soldiers who raided German trenches. (NLS)

Somme	23/4/16	Captain Hammonds returned to duty. A Rest Day on account of Infantry relief. Cleaning wagons and billets etc.	
Somme (near Bethune)	3/5/16	Work on Royal Army Medical Corps dressing station was completed. Infantry working parties now increased to about 700 men.	NSAH
	12/5/16	About 12 shells were fired into Company billets. 5 were duds. Shrapnel size was about 4-7 inches. No damage was done and no one was hurt.	
	19/5/16	Company commenced to join up islands 11 and 11a by trench boards along ISLAND LINE at head of LOOP ROAD. Reached COVER TRENCH at the head of PIONEER ROAD. Commenced laying trench boards.	
	20/5/16	Sapper Furlonger was killed by rifle bullet in LOOP ROAD. Work commenced again on ISLANDS 11 and 11a.	
Somme	24/5/16	Water supply from LE PLANTAIN to Old BRITISH LINE almost finished.	NASH
	25/5/16	Rest Day. Church service for Company held at LE TOURET. 118th Brigade took over the line.	
Somme (near Bethune)	29/5/16	B174 Battery gun pits and billets completed. Also billets in RUE LE PINETTE. Work on the observation post at LE PLANTIN was stopped due to shells having destroyed the wall in front of the post.	
Le Touret	1/6/16	Rest day. One Light Draught (LD) Horse impaled itself on a picket stake and had to be shot. Inter Battalion Relief.	
	4/6/16	Commenced erecting steel dug outs for A174 Battery and all old work proceeded with.	
	6/6/16	Commenced with new tram line joining up PIONEER and BARNTON ROAD trenches.	
Le Touret	8/6/16	Commenced machine gun emplacement at junction of FIFE ROAD and OLD BRITISH LINE firing north, plus also French mortar dug outs in COVER TRENCH. Due to excessively wet weather, night work had to be abandoned.	

Scottish Soldiers moving up to the Frontline. (IWM)

LONDON SCOTTISH GOING TO THEIR TRENCHES

26.

Daily Mail War Pictures

The use of aerial photography

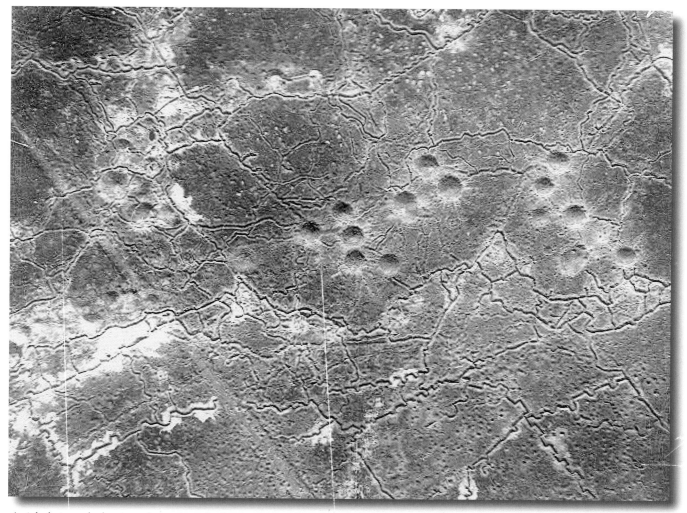

Aerial photograph showing what a network of extensive trench systems looked like. (Taken near Arras, June 1916. Arras is 25 miles to the north of Thiepval, where Charlie Robeson was soon to be fighting. Massive shell holes are clearly seen). (IWM)

Somme	9/6/16	Joined up ISLANDS No 10a and 11. Also connected ISLANDS No1 to No 9 rendering them capable of being held. ADVANCED BRIGADE HEADQUARTERS completed.	NSAH
(near Bethune)	18/6/16	Sapper R. W. Thomas was killed by rifle fire, working between 9 and 10 ISLANDS and buried in BRITISH CEMETERY at LE TOURET.	NSAH
(between Bethune & Arras)	23/6/16	Lt J. B. Wilkinson was shot through the head about 1am, between ISLANDS 9 and 10. Died of his wounds at No 33 casualty clearing station (CCS) BETHUNE at 8.15 am. 101124 Sapper Hazelton F. was alas wounded, shot in the chest and evacuated to the 134th FIELD AMBULANCE. ISLANDS 11 and 12 joined up.	
	27/6/16	BARNTON ROAD trench and BARNTON RAILWAY were shelled rather heavily. All repairs were carried out immediately.	

Somme (near Bethune)	28/6/16	Completed observation post for A179 BATTERY at DRESSING STATION at RUE De CAILLOUX. Also observation post for ADVANCED BRIGADE HQ. Very heavy rain flooded all communication trenches and owing to the rapid rise of water in all streams and ditches the pumps were of little use.
	30/6/16	Continued pumping communication trenches, weather turning finer. Pumps taking effect but water levels very high everywhere. Major N. S. A Harrison OC 225th Field Company RE
Le Touret	2/7/16	Major N. S. A Harrison went on Special Leave. D H H

British artillery shelling German positions at the Front (IWM)

4/7/16   Description of the Raid on German Trenches (BETHUNE combined map sheet 1:40,000) –

1. **Object of Raid –** To enter German trenches when they had been cleared by the infantry and to demolish them as much as possible. In particular, to destroy 2 machine gun emplacements reported to be at (13) and (C) (Map positions).

2. **Arrangement of parties –** 1 Officer, 2 Non Commissioned Officers (NCOs) and 14 sappers, from No 3 Section to accompany the Infantry party which consisted of about 200 officers and other ranks of the 16th Battalion RIFLE BRIGADE. The Sapper detachment was subdivided into 4 squads of 3 and 1 spare squad. Each squad carried a specially prepared box containing 32 slabs of gun cotton, a light table with adjustable legs for supporting the charge against the roof of a dug out, a hand lamp and detonator etc.

3. **Plan of operation –** The raid was practised on a full sized model of the German Trenches. The detachment was to enter at Point (A) as soon as the Infantry reported that the trenches were clear up to point (E) and (F). Two squads were then to proceed to the left and two to the right, place their charges in the most suitable position and then retire.

4. **The actual operation –** Weather cloudy with little rain and little wind. At 11.30am there was an artillery bombardment on German Front Line and continued for an hour. At 12.30pm, first Infantry assaulted (A3 b24) but retired on meeting heavy rifle fire. This disorganised the rehearsed plan and although the infantry subsequently assaulted again and got into the German Trenches, the original plan could not be fully carried out.

At 12.50pm (approximately), the infantry sent backwards for the Engineers. The whole detachment with all men ran across and entered the trench at (A). Lt Scott with Sgt Myers with Sappers Besant, English, Himsworth, Duffy, Windross and Maughan went to the left and 2nd Cpl Murdy with sappers Bartley, Butler, Doe, Robson, Symonds, Moss, Nichols and Brown A, went to the right.

Of the left half, Sapper Besant (wounded in shoulder), Windross, Duffy and Maughan, returned about 20 minutes later and reported that Lt Scott having placed his charge had told the others to clear, as he was lighting the fuse. The remainder of the Company has not been heard of since.

The right half of the detachment was unable to make any headway along the trench as it was full of men fighting hand-to-hand. They were ordered to withdraw by the Major of the Infantry who was in charge of the raid and did so without casualties except that Spr Barley fell on a metal screw stake. 2nd Cpl Murdy showed good spirit on his return and gave a clear account of what he saw.

5. **Information –** The German Trenches were narrow and on average 8 feet deep (4ft to 5ft below ground level).They were wet at the bottom and apparently only kept habitable by electric pumps, two of which were seen. Revetment was mostly brushwood and in some cases very high, as it allowed for a kneeling position. The dug out in which Lt. Scott placed the charge was low and had a concrete roof. It is uncertain whether the charge went off or not. The dug-out was in the back of the trench and was certainly not a machine gun emplacement.

Remainder of Company – The Officer Commanding Headquarters, was in CONVENT observation post. Lt Scobie with 8 men in No 1 Section was in charge of the LE PLANTIN tramway. Lt Argent with the whole of No 2 Section was in charge of BARNTON TRAMWAY. Lt Heavisides with 6 men of No 4 Section was in charge of KINGS CROSS TRAMWAY. Each Section patrolled their respective lines and had material to repair any damage. Bricklayers were also ready with material for repairing observation posts and 2 plumbers were ready to repair pipe lines. The enemy however did very little retaliation and no damage was caused. The whole Company except the 4 missing men were back in billets by 5am. At night, all work was carried on as usual.

D. H. Hammonds

Capt. RE

Tracing of aeroplane photograph of German trenches

Below is a drawing made from an aerial photograph, taken on 5th May 1916, of German trenches to be attacked by the 225th Field Company, on a raid described in the War Diaries on the 4th July 1916. Signed by D. H. Hammonds

(National Archives)

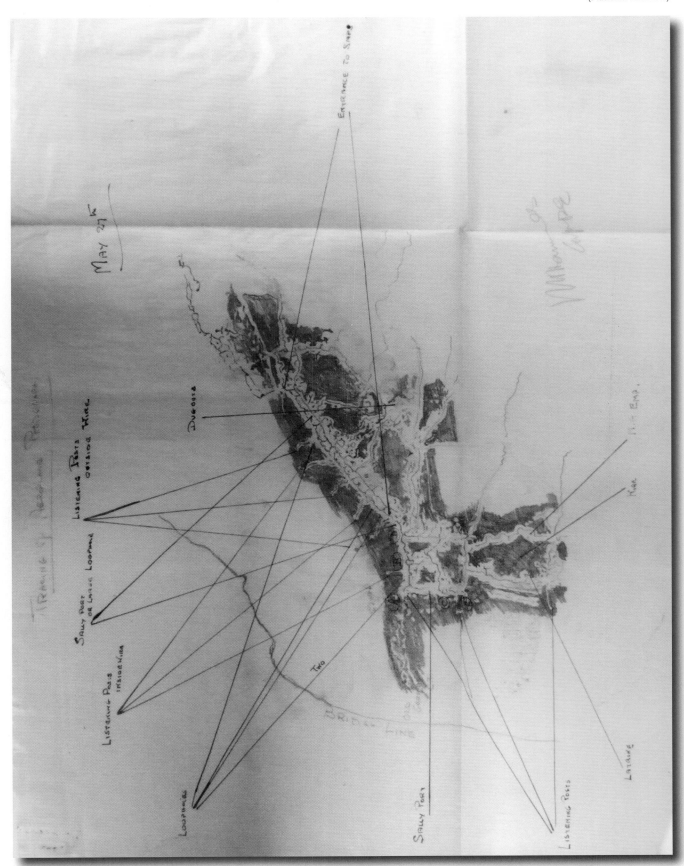

	19/7/16	Major N. S. A Harrison returned from leave. The day workers were recalled at 12 noon and stood ready to move at 1 hours notice, until 6pm. This was on account of XI Corps attack in the north.	
Somme	21/7/16	Extension of BARNTON TRAMWAY to BARNTON TEE was ordered by Division and started at once with party of West Country Yeomanry. L.Cpl. Reeves was wounded by bullet in leg.	DHH
	26/7/16	Observation post at LE PLANTIN was heavily shelled and badly damaged and rendered useless. Sapper J. F. Barton was killed at 12.30am and Sapper N. S. Robinson wounded at the same time and place.	

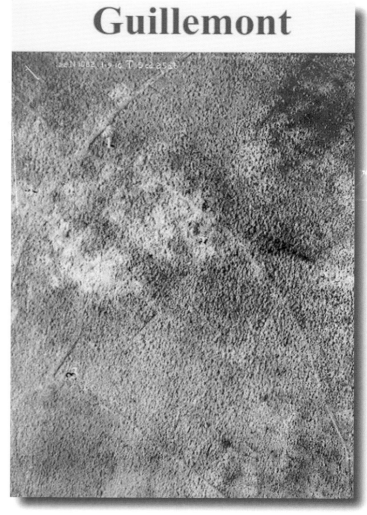

Two aerial photographs showing the effects of heavy shelling on the town of Guillemont on the Somme, in July and again in September 1916 (IWM).

	29/7/16	Lt Scobie killed at 10.15pm when out on reconnaissance in front of the wire in preparation for raid to be held the following night.	
	30/7/16	A raid was attempted from ISLAND 3 in which the Company was to place 3 BANGALORE TORPEDOES and explode them electrically under the German wire. Owing to the death of Lt Scobie this had to be carried out without reconnaissance. The party failed to reach the enemy wire in time and were unable to place the torpedoes in position.	
Somme	31/7/16	One of the torpedoes left out in NO MANS LAND was safely recovered. A considerable amount of shell fire was experienced on this front but no great damage was done. N. S. A Harrison, Major OC 225th Field Company RE	
	2/8/16	The 225th Field Company were relieved by the 227th Field company in the FESTUBERT Area. The 225th taking over all work in the GIVENCHY area. Since the Company landed in France exactly 5 months ago they have been engaged in nothing but FRONT LINE work, all of it night work.	NSAH
	5/8/16	Company erected 4 bomb stores at FENSHAWE CASTLE and GIVENCHY trenches and carried on with works on machine gun posts, pontooning and rapid wiring.	
Somme	6/8/16	No 4 section erected a platform in the square at BETHUNE for the purpose of a service to commemorate the 2nd anniversary of the start of the war. Company attended the service and dismantled the platform.	
Gauchy -a-la-Tour	10/8/16	Company moved off from billets at 6.30am to GAUCHY-A-LA-TOUR.	
Marguay	11/8/16	Company marched to MARGUAY, arriving at 7.30pm.	
Rocourt en Leau	12/8/16	Company moved to ROCOURT EN LEAU arriving at 7.30pm. Company had to be billeted in the fields as no billets were available in the village.	NSAH
	15/8/16	A route march was undertaken in the morning, about 12 miles. In the afternoon feet inspection took place.	

Postcards sent to Charlie in France from home, during the summer of 1916

Springwood Estate Gates, Kelso. (Authors collection)

Trinity United Free Church, Kelso. (Authors collection)

Living conditions in the trenches

'Trench maps drawn at the time often show a number of lines of trenches criss-crossing the length of the Front Line. There were forward trenches, second line trenches, reserve line and communication trenches. Front Line trenches were defended from enemy trenches (sometimes as little as 100 metres away) by row upon row of barbed wire. In front of the wire was 'no-man's land'. This was an area of ground which was a killing zone. It was a place that favoured the defenders not the attackers.

On arrival at the Front Line, the Royal Engineers and infantry would either occupy existing trenches or more often than not, dig new ones. Food was carried from reserve positions, through a series of supply trenches. Warm food would be carried in wooden boxes filled with hay to keep it warm. Very little food was warm by the time it reached the Front Line. Tea was regularly brewed up in small stoves along the length of trench systems. The main food supplied to the soldiers was bread, which could be anything up to a week old. Tinned corned beef (bully beef) was a staple as was jam. 'Maconochie' was eaten too. It was tinned stew comprising meat and vegetables and affectionately known by the men by its manufacturer's name, 'Conner'.

Food parcels from home were eagerly awaited and shared around pals. Mail supplies were very regular and men were encouraged to write home. Many men smoked cigarettes, which were subsidised by the army, as a tobacco allowance. Boredom could be a big problem amongst the men. In reserve trenches, men were kept busy with regular kit inspections, drill and cleaning of equipment.

Between major attacks there were smaller localised attacks. There was the constant threat from shelling, sniper fire, gas attacks and shrapnel bombs. Anyone inquisitive enough to stick their head above ground level often became a focus for enemy machine gun fire. Short raids by a small number of men were regularly carried out as a way of gaining intelligence about enemy strength. Prisoners were often taken, as they could be a useful source of information regarding enemy intentions.

Keeping clean was almost impossible in trench life. It was common to spend three weeks at a time in a forward position before being relieved to a reserve position for rest, a change of clothes and a bath. Latrines were often dug in front of forward trenches (below ground level) and were never a pleasant experience.

Men in the front line trenches regularly exchanged daily shelling and machine gun fire, which would start before dawn. Unusually heavy shelling by the enemy was often a prelude to an imminent infantry attack. Gas masks were carried by all soldiers in front line positions and when on attack. Chlorine and mustard gas would blow down wind and flow down into enemy trenches, where it gathered as a deadly cloud, burning exposed skin, particularly the nose, mouth and throat. Poison gas maimed soldiers by the score.'

(Source - BBC History)

Life in the trenches

A German trench. Men shared the trenches with rats…lots of rats. (IWM).

German soldiers checking their shirts for lice whilst another soldier keeps a look out. (IWM).

Hot stew at meal time in British trenches. (NLS)

British soldiers in a flooded communication trench. (NLS)

Trench Foot

In British trenches, regular feet inspections were essential to prevent trench foot. Trench foot formed when men stood in cold muddy water for days on end. Their feet would swell up and become infected. It was extremely painful. (IWM)

Somme	18/8/16	Physical exercises, section drill and use of Weldon trestle in morning. Demolition training and map reading in the afternoon.
Vitermont	23–27/8/16	Moved to SIBIVILLE, to SUS-S-LEQUER, to BOIS Du WERNIMONT to VITERMONT .
Auchon-villers	28/8/16	Erection of barbed wire entanglements for prisoners. The trestle wagon was ran into by a train taking working party to the trenches. It was smashed to pieces.

Charlie's Division is moved south to near Thiepval Ridge

Trench maps were produced by all armies fighting during the war. Detailed maps were essential if the enemy was to be beaten. Aerial photography was in its infancy but played an important role in ensuring new trenches were dug in the right place and at the appropriate distance from the enemy trenches.

Trench map of the British Front Line near Beaumont Hamel in July 1916
(Note - Map not be carried into the attack or on patrol)

The War Diary entries from 7th–10th September 1916 has Charlie and the 225th Field Company fighting on the Frontline, from trenches at CLONMEL AVENUE, TIPPERARY AVENUE, THURLES DUMP and PICCADILLY. The trenches are clearly visible on the official trench map of Beaumont Hamel of July 1916. The dark blue lines are British trenches and the light blue lines are German trenches. Beaumont Hamel was not captured by the British Army until mid November 1916, towards the very end of the 1916 Somme Campaign.

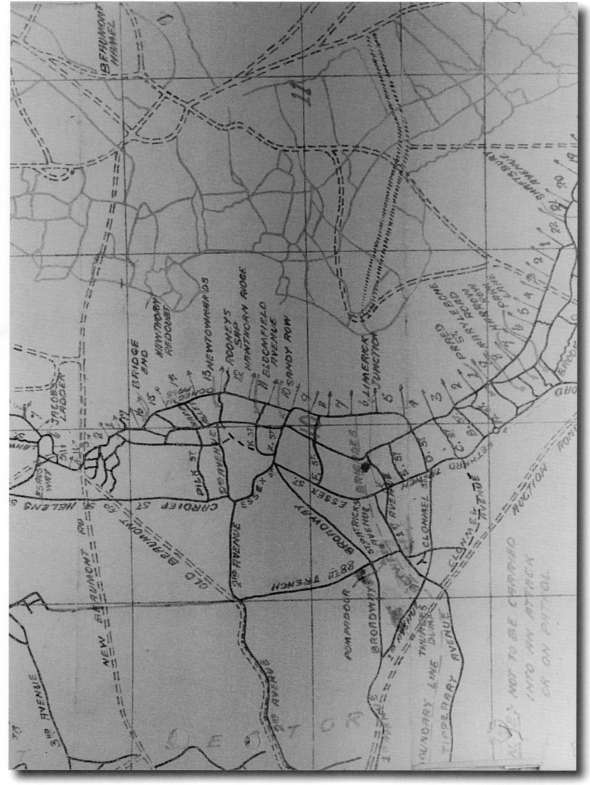

(National Archives)

Transporting men around the battlefield

On their way - Narrow gauge railways were used extensively for transporting troops. (NLS)

| Auchon-villers | 1/9/16 | Part of billets heavily bombarded for one hour wounding one man, killing 2 horses, destroying the front portion of a tool cart, including tools, a good deal of kit and clothing and a bicycle. |

The attack on Thiepval Ridge, Stuff Trench and the Schwaben Redoubt

The Battle of Thiepval Ridge was the first large offensive mounted by the British Reserve Army of Lieutenant General Hubert Gough. The objective laid out by British Commander Douglas Haig was to push the Germans off the high ground of the Thiepval Ridge including the heavily fortified Schwaben Redoubt. 230 heavy guns and 570 field guns were used in the assault. (The Schwaben Redoubt lies between the Thiepval Memorial and the Ulster Tower today.) It was a German strongpoint consisting of a mass of gun emplacements, trenches and tunnels. The Cambridgeshire Regiment (39th Division) assaulted and successfully captured the Schwaben Redoubt. The Redoubt was of great strategic importance and had been fought over many times with great loss of life. The success was so phenomenal that General Haig recounted the attack as being "one of the finest feats of arms in the history of the British Army". (www.wikipedia.org)

Vitermont	3/9/16	The 116th and 117th Brigades attacked the enemy FRONT LINE north of THIEPVAL. The 225th Field Company were in reserve. In the evening the whole Company went up into the trenches repairing the same. No enemy trenches were captured.	
Thiepval	4/9/16	Repaired trenches in 39th Division area but very little was done owing to an extraordinarily heavy bombardment of gas shells and the wounded constantly passing along the trenches.	NSAH
Somme	5/9/16	Continued work at night, repairing the trenches particularly GORDON and BEDFORD ROAD trench but work considerably hampered by bad weather.	
	7/9/16	Carried on with 2 deep dugouts in BROOK STREET trench and one in PICCADILLY trench. Cleared CLONMEL AVENUE to ST JOHNS ROAD junction. 200 yards in ST JOHNS ROAD and 400 yards in TIPPERARY AVENUE. Weather was fine and a large amount of work was done.	
	10/9/16	Repaired tramline between THURLES DUMP and UXBRIDGE ROAD trench where it was destroyed by shell fire.	
Somme	16/9/16	Continued laying trench boards for all trenches in left sector. Laid a further 100 yards of rails on the tramway extensions.	
Thiepval	26/9/16	Major N. S. A Harrison handed over command of Company to Captain D. H. Hammonds. Major Harrison was evacuated to the Field Ambulance as immediately unfit for active service.	
Somme	26/9/16	Work on the trenches was stopped. The Brigade was 'standing to' in order to support an attack on the right flank. The Company stood by waiting for orders.	
	27/9/16	Company still 'standing by' on account of the attack on THIEPVAL.	
Somme	30/9/16	Company area shelled in the evening. Driver Walton J. G. killed and Bell V. C. and Tyler F. L. wounded. D. H. Hammonds Capt. RE OC 225th Fld Coy	
Martinsart	6/10/16	Started repair to ENNISKILLEN trench. A new trench was taped out towards the old German line north of THIEPVAL.	
Thiepval	7/10/16	No 4 RE Section and infantry party failed to dig the ENNISKILLEN EXTENSION last night owing to heavy shell fire. No 3 Section started sapping from Point 91 to old GERMAN LINE and completed 30 yards chiefly by joining shell holes together.	
Somme	8/10/16	Party again failed to dig ENNISKILLEN EXTENSION owing to heavy shell fire last night. Sapper Leddy W was wounded. Lt. L. A. Dibden arrived from ROUEN.	DHH
Martinsart	12/10/16	No infantry parties arrived owing to proposed attack on SCHWABEN REDOUBT. Attack postponed. Work carried on by sappers as far as possible.	
	14/10/16	No infantry parties arrived owing to the attack on the SCHWABEN REDOUBT.	

Zero Hour

British Infantry preparing for the attack. An attack would normally occur around dawn. The artillery bombardment would cease and the men would be given a tot of rum before 'going over the top' (NLS).

The Whistle Blows

'Going over the top'. (NLS).

German machine gun posts took a heavy toll on British infantry. Slaughter was inevitable but the British High Command persisted with infantry attacks against heavily fortified German positions. (IWM).

Thiepval	15/10/16	The Company was ordered to consolidate the gains on left flank of new FRONT captured in yesterdays attack. Two strong points made at points 45 and 86 in shifts, by all available sappers. Sapper Crozier G, killed by shell fire on way back from work.
Somme	16/1016	Carried on with above strong points. No 86 was completely obliterated by shell fire during the night.

Effect of shell fire on Delville wood near Guillemont. Very few features above ground survived heavy shelling. The only relative safety was to be found underground (NLS).

	18/10/16	PAISLEY AVENUE cleared up to TANK STREET trench.	
Thiepval	19/10/16	Billets heavily shelled during the night and one dugout was blown in causing the following casualties: Driver Hunter G F, killed, Driver Movel E W, wounded. Pioneer Dobbs J H, wounded. 1 Light Draught, (LD) horse killed and 1 LD horse wounded. 1 LD Mule wounded.	
Somme	24/10/16	Sappers dug 50 yards of new trench on left side of OLD GERMAN FRONT LINE. The infantry did very little owing to the state of the ground. The mud was so sticky that some of the men lost their boots.	DHH

Some progress at last

British soldiers happy to have gained some ground. (NLS).

Somme	25/10/16	No 1 Section completed the work of preparing a trench for the tanks. This track was marked with white tape and the worst inequalities in the ground levelled off.

Tanks were used in battle for the first time, in July 1916 on the Somme. Most of the tanks quickly became bogged down and were abandoned (IWM).

Tanks had a very limited (mostly psychological) effect during the early war. They did become effective weapons but many succumbed to the mud (NLS).

	27/10/16	Company carried out trench boarding at point 91.
Thiepval	30/10/16	Very heavy rain interfered with work but some progress was made with more trench boarding.
Somme	7/11/16	Very heavy rain but fair progress made with clearing dugouts and digging out WHITECHURCH STREET (a support line).
	9/11/16	Carried on clearing out FRONT LINE and SUPPORT LINE trenches north of THIEPVAL WOOD.
	12/11/16	Sgt. Rawley and six men went down and cleared MILL ROAD. They found only a few wire obstructions.
	12/11/16	No 1 Section, under 2nd Lt. Holley, marched out at 10pm to join the 1/1st HERTS for the attack the next day. They marched to assembly position in THIEPVAL.
Somme	12/11/16	Lnc. Cpl. Hodgson and 6 men of No 3 Section went out with purpose of searching for mines in the dugouts at ST PIERRE DIVION.

*A shell bursting on a
frontline trench. (NLS).*

British soldiers within a few yards of Thiepval village. (NLS).

Fighting and more fighting – It seemed never ending

An exhausted British soldier catches some sleep within 100yds of Thiepval village. (NLS)

Charlie with the 39th Division attack and capture the Schwaben Redoubt near Thiepval

Thiepval	12/11/16	Lt. Dibden in charge of tracks for tanks up PAISLEY VALLEY. He was present at 6pm when tanks moved off and remained until 1.00am assisting and guiding.	DHH
Somme	13/11/16	Zero hour for attack on ST PIERRE DIVION was 5.45am. Capt. D. H. Hammonds, Lt. Argent and Lt. Newman were all ill in bed with influenza or fever. Cpl. Hodgson returned at 11.00am and reported that he had searched all German dugouts in ST PIERRE DIVION and had taken wire from several but had found no trace of any mines. Cleared portions of the HANSA line and made firing bays which were immediately occupied by the Infantry.	

The targets for Charlie and the 225th Field Company on 13th November 1916, were German soldiers in trenches at St. Pierre Divion and the Schwaben Redoubt at Thiepval, which is visible on this trench map (upper centre) dated July 1916.

The British Frontline is marked in dark black hatch. The light red lines are German trenches. Beaumont Hamel, Thiepval and the infamous Schwaben Redoubt all fell to the British Army by mid November 1916 after five intense months of brutal conflict and significant loss of life on both sides. It was the men of Charlie's 39th Division that finally took the Schwaben Redoubt.

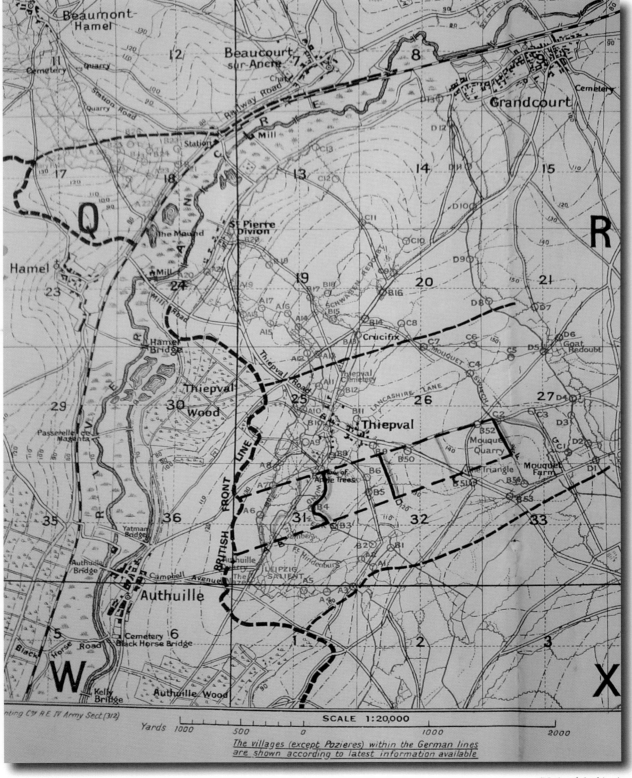

(National Archives)

The impregnable German held stronghold of the Schwaben Redoubt

When viewed from the air, the mighty defensive trench system surrounding the Schwaben Redoubt (centre top) is clear to see. (Wikipedia.org)

Early in the battle of July 1916. This is the view South East towards the Schwaben Redoubt, (beyond the village of Hamel), that Charlie and the 39th Division would have witnessed during the third week of November 1916. By late November, all the trees and houses had been completely destroyed. After the successful attacks on Thiepval Ridge (marked by smoke rising at the top right of the picture), the Schwaben Redoubt (marked by shells exploding at top left of picture) was finally taken by the men of Charlie's Division. (Wikipedia.org)

The Battle for the Schwaben Redoubt was a ferocious encounter for Charlie and the men of the 39th Division in mid November 1916. (Bridgeman Education).

Due to the persistent determination of British soldiers, including those of the 39th Division, the Germans were finally driven from the Schwaben Redoubt by the end of November 1916. This engagement effectively ended the Battle of the Somme in 1916. (Bridgeman Education).

The following is an account of the attack by the 39th Division on the Schwaben Redoubt during the on-going Battle of Ancre, which took place between 13th-18th November (extracted from 'The Somme – The Day by Day Account' by Chris McCarthy)

'On the 13th November, the 39th Division attacked on the right with the 118th Brigade. They formed up in no man's land on tape guides laid by the 234th Field Company Royal Engineers, unnoticed by the Germans. The 1/1st Hertfords, facing north, had the Hansa line as their objective and had reached it by 7.00am. The 1/1st Cambridgeshires attacked northwest, reaching Mill Trench with little difficulty and by 10.00am, the station crossing at Beaumont Mill (point where they would later meet the 63rd Division) was secured. The 1/6th Cheshires and 4/5th Black Watch were handicapped by fog and lost direction in the maze of trenches. At 6.15am the 16th Sherwood Foresters (117th Brigade), attacking from Mill Road up the Ancre valley near the river on the left of the Corps, surprised the enemy. Two Companies were to clear the dugouts in the banks of the river and one along the top of the bank. They met a company of Black Watch who joined in the final assault on St Pierre Divion which fell to the mixed forces of Foresters, Highlanders and Cheshires at 7.40am. Of the 3 tanks that were scheduled to start from Thiepval and aid the assault, one was lost to the mud before reaching Thiepval and another had mechanical trouble. The third reached the German Front Line at 7.00am but shortly fell into dugout and was attacked. It sent a pigeon for help. The Foresters and Black Watch arrived at 9.00am and drove off the attackers.

Stranded tank crew sending out a pigeon with a message for assistance. (IWM).

At 11.30am the 13th November, the 11th Hampshires (attached to 116th Brigade), who were waiting in the dugouts of the Schwaben Redoubt, advanced down the Ancre Valley, only to be withdrawn that afternoon. The Hertfords were digging-in 50yds beyond the Hansa Line, with the 7th Royal North Lancs (56th Brigade) on their right. The Cambridgeshires and Cheshires worked on Mill Trench as far back as St. Pierre Divion which was organised for defence. All units then consolidated. A section of the 4th Motor Machinegun Battalion with some guns on side-cars drove down the Ancre via Mill Road and then manhandled forward. 118th Brigade was responsible for the defence of the ground gained and set the Hertfords to construct a redoubt at the junction of Mill Trench and Hansa Line. The Cambridgeshires dug a support line facing north across the base of the Hertford's position. The Cheshires were made responsible for St. Pierre Divion and the strong points in the river valley and also the posts at the Mill east of Beucourt Station. The Black Watch who were muddled up with the Cheshires were ordered to reform and occupy the right of the Hansa Line. At 6.45pm, two small counter-attacks on the Hertford's position were fought off. At 8.52am, by which time all the objectives had been taken, the 227th Field Company RE and part of the 13th Gloucesters (Pioneers) were to repair the Hamel-St. Pierre Divion road and by 4pm a mud track was laid to the village.

On 14th November the 39th Division finally drove the last of the Germans out of the Schwaben Redoubt with the 4/5th Black Watch, 1/1st Cambridgeshires (118th Brigade) and the 17th Kings Royal Rifle Company (117th Brigade). The fighting lasted until 11pm. The 1/6th Cheshires (118th Brigade) advanced the line on the left. Three counter attacks made the next day, two with flame throwers were repulsed.'

On the 14th November, the 51st Highland Division (also part of General Gough's 5th Army) was fighting 2km to the north west of the 39th Division at Thiepval. After a very long hard fight lasting 5 months, they finally succeeded in capturing Beaumont Hamel.

The Germans withdrew from battle. General Haig now closed down the battlefield on the Somme and refocused his attention at Ypres Salient in Flanders, Belgium. Charlie's Division was immediately moved to Canal Bank, Ypres.

One of many shell dumps of empty shell cases, along the roadside in the Frontline Area. (NLS).

Men grabbed rest when they could.

British soldiers sleeping in a captured enemy trench. A look-out was always posted. (IWM).

Winnie continued to send postcards through the autumn of 1916

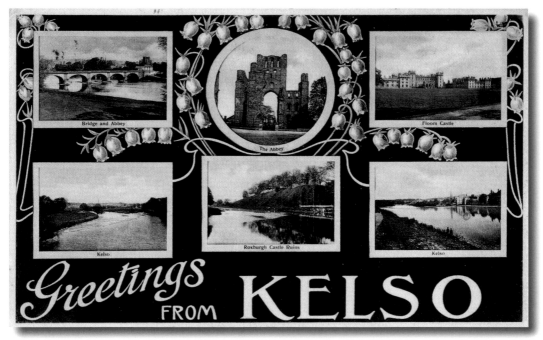

Photo montage of Kelso.   (Authors collection)

River Tweed below the Junction Pool, Kelso.   (Authors collection)

Somme	14/11/16	Received orders to march under 116th Brigade to WARLOY. Marched off at 2pm and billeted at CANTOY about 9 miles march.
Cantoy	15/11/16	Marched off at 9.30am to HEM. 17 miles march.

SCOTTISH TROOPS CROSSING PONTOON BRIDGE IN FRANCE   *Active Service, No 3*

Scottish Soldiers on the move with Royal Engineers Pontoon Bridging team alongside. (IWM).

Hem	18/11/16	Marched off at 1.45pm to DOULLENS station and entrained. Detrained at HOPOUTRE siding at 3pm. Marched to Z camp at POPERINGE **(near Ypres, Belgium)**.

Towards the end of 1916, Charlie Robeson and the 225th Field Company Royal Engineers moved with the rest of the 39th Division to Ypres, Belgium. They dug in on the Canal Bank and found there a stalemate battlefield situation, like the one they had just left on the Somme. Charlie fought at the Ypres Salient throughout 1917. Mud and rain came to symbolise life on the battlefields at what became known collectively as 'Passchendaele'.

Arrival on the battlefield at Passchendaele			
Poperingue	19/11/16	The Company took up completion of construction of Z and Y camps. Erecting Nissan Huts of various description.	DHH
Ypres	20–23/11/16	Lt West and Lt Kingsworth joined the Company. Infantry class of 10 officers and 30 other ranks (OR) arrived for instruction in field works.	
	30/11/16	The Instruction class completed their course and finished up with a written exam. The outdoor work of this class was very satisfactory throughout but the written exam results were poor chiefly owing to the lack of education amongst the men. Four of them could not read or write. At 8.30pm we received orders to take over from 151st Field Company on 1st Dec. Issued orders to march at 10am.	DHH

Digging in at Canal Bank, Ypres, Belgium

Ypres occupied a strategic position during World War I because it stood in the path of Germany's planned sweep across the rest of Belgium and into France from the north. Of the battles fought, the largest, best-known and most costly in human suffering was the Third Battle of Ypres (21st July to 6th November 1917, also known as the Battle of Passchendaele), in which the British, Canadians, ANZAC, and French forces recaptured the Passchendaele Ridge east of Ypres, at a terrible cost in lives. After months of fighting, this battle resulted in nearly half a million casualties to both sides and only a few miles of ground was won by Allied forces. During the course of the war, Ypres was all but obliterated by the artillery fire. The weather played a significant role with men fighting knee deep in mud for months on end. During the first half of 1917 the 39th Division spent time consolidating their position at Canal Bank, Ypres and digging new trench systems. They were preparing the ground for a major new offensive in the summer of 1917. They would fight their way to a small town called 'Passchendaele'. (www.wikipedia.org)

Poperingue	1/12/16	The Company marched off at 10.00am to 117th Company HQ. Halted there until 4pm. Marched then to forward billets at YSER CANAL (Ypres) arriving at 6.45pm. No 1 Section with Lt. Kingsnorth, remained at transport lines. Lt. Carroll with 151st Company remained at forward billets. 2 infantry officers and 100 men were attached to Company for work. Worked on draining and deepening the trenches.	
Ypres	4–12/12/16	Fitted box respirators (including a test in gas chamber) to 2, 3 and 4 Sections. Carried on with deepening and draining trenches.	
	14/12/16	Commenced construction of railway from CLIFFORD TOWERS to TURCO.	
Yser Canal	15–24/12/16	Carried on with railway construction from AUSTERLITZ to TURCO. Captain D. H. Hammonds returned from leave.	
Ypres	25/12/16	Christmas Day. No work today owing to 118th Brigade being attached to the Company. Lt West evacuated to Field Ambulance having been rejected by the medical board as being unfit for service in FRONT LINE.	
	28/12/16	Act. Capt. Argent went back to the horse lines to supervise work on gunners stables.	DHH

D. H. Hammonds Capt. RE
Officer Commanding, 225th Field Company.

Postcards home at Christmas 1916

THERE'S A LONG, LONG TRAIL (1).

Nights are growing very lonely, days are very long,
I'm a-growing weary, only list'ning for your song;
Old remembrances are thronging thro' my memory,
Throinging till it seems the world is full of dreams,
Just to call you back to me.

BAMFORTH COPYRIGHT.   WORDS BY PERMISSION OF WEST & CO., OXFORD STREET. W.

Charlie continued to send letters and postcards home.
Letters, cards and food parcels from home meant
everything to the soldiers at the Front. Christmas
was a particularly difficult time for them.

(Authors collection)

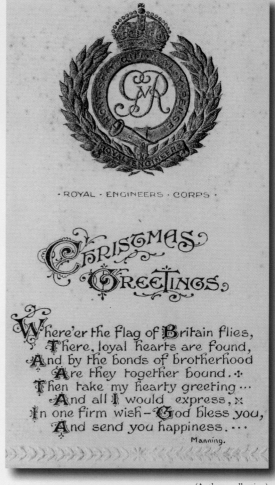

· ROYAL · ENGINEERS · CORPS ·

Christmas
Greetings

Where'er the flag of Britain flies,
There, loyal hearts are found,
And by the bonds of brotherhood
Are they together bound.
Then take my hearty greeting
And all I would express,
In one firm wish – God bless you,
And send you happiness.

Manning.

(Authors collection)

A silk Christmas card sent by Charlie Robeson to Winnie in Kelso, in December 1916.

Christmas Day rest was short lived with shells bursting at night on frontline positions. (NLS).

A field service postcard to Kelso in January 1917

Below is an example of a Field Service post card, which was used by soldiers to inform friends and family back home that they were OK. This one was sent by Mr H. E. Stewart, to friends at Taits Solicitors office in Kelso, on 15th January 1917. The message on the reverse, simply states that he is alive and quite well. Soldiers weren't allowed to say any more, for fear of giving away vital information to the enemy, if the cards were intercepted. The Red Cross letter was sent on 26th April 1917 to the same address.

Field Service postcards and Red Cross letter to Taits solicitors, in Kelso.

The Year 1917: Ypres, Passchendaele and the mud of Flanders, Belgium

Summary of the progress of war during 1917

'The course of the war changed dramatically during 1917 and the Germans began to gain the upper hand. The German Commander Ludendorff made a strategic decision to withdraw to a predetermined and heavily fortified line, called the Hindenburg Line. This was to give his forces time to regroup. On the Eastern Front, the Germans had some successes that contributed to the Russian Revolution. This revolution brought down the Tsar of Russia. Russia became a Communist state under Lenin in October of that year. From late 1917, the German forces were able to move more men and equipment to the Western Front. German hopes were high, that the British would quickly succumb to overwhelming pressure. This did not happen because at the same time as Germany was declaring a propaganda war on Britain, they were doing the same to America, by trying to entice Mexico to invade the USA. This backfired and on 6th April, America came directly into the war, on the side of the Allies. This was hugely significant, as it provided the Allies with much needed men, ships, guns and ammunition. The Americans were also able to lend money to the British and French Governments, to buy more food and supplies.

The British, however, were still suffering in France and at the battle of Arras in April 1917, they sustained huge losses. In July, at Ypres (Passchendaele), mustard gas was used by the Germans with devastating effect. British casualties were horrific, with little new ground gained. In November, at Cambrai, the British used a large number of tanks for a mass attack for the first time. A significant amount of new territory was gained here and the German front line was pushed back some way. The Germans quickly regrouped however and made a counter offensive, which retook much of the ground the British had just gained.

Beyond Europe, British forces and the Allies, were making significant territorial gains against the enemy. In Spring 1917, in the Middle East for example, T H Lawrence, 'Lawrence of Arabia', helped co-ordinate an Arab attack on Akaba and by late 1918, the Ottoman Empire had agreed to a ceasefire. On the high seas, submarine patrols were having a severe impact on ships travelling alone, which were carrying food supplies to Britain. Much allied shipping was being sunk. Ships began to travel in groups (convoys) with a military escort. Food however still had to be rationed. Meat, lard, butter, margarine and sugar became tradable commodities. Chocolate became a luxury, as did fresh fruit. Because men were in short supply at home, the Women's Army Auxiliary Corps was formed, putting women into military operations (though not fighting positions) for the first time. By early 1918, the Royal Flying Corps became the Royal Air Force. Women flew planes from factories where they were made, to airfields for distribution. Anti-German feeling had become such a problem at home in Britain, that the British Royal Family changed their surname to Windsor to appear more British.'

(Source - BBC History).

Passchendaele – The Battles of Ypres, Belgium 1917

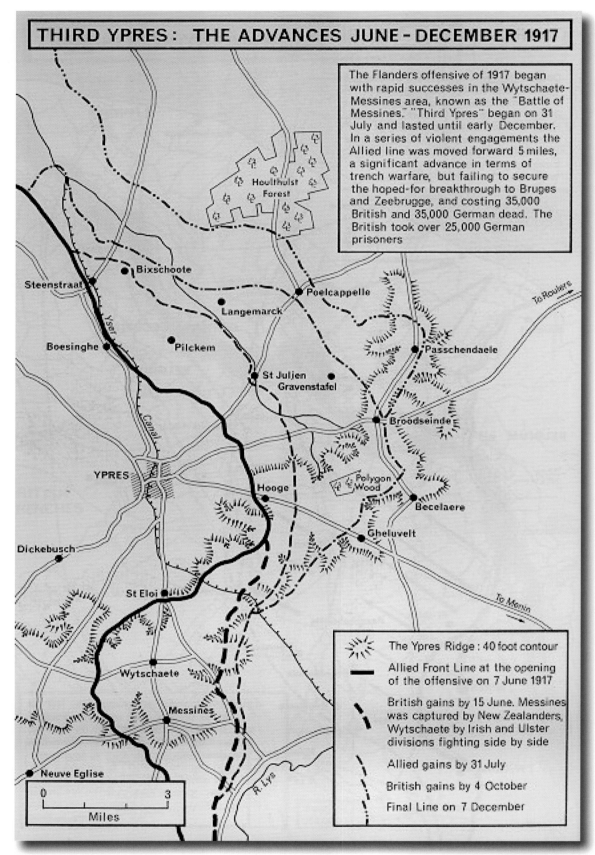

Map showing the British advance at Ypres from June- December 1917. Charlie Robeson and the Engineers dug in on the Canal Bank at Ypres before fighting in most of the major battles of 1917 at Pilckem Ridge, Langemarck, Menin Road Ridge, Polygon Wood and Passchendaele. (www.gutenburg.org).

Charlie and the 39th Division's location, during the first half of 1917

From January to June 1917, the 39th Division RE worked on digging trenches and laying mines in the Ypres area of Belgium. This was in preparation for a major offensive later in the year. Both the Germans and the British were exhausted after the stalemate on the Somme. It took until the summer of 1917 before either side was ready for a major engagement. In June 1917, ahead of the British offensive, a series of 19 massive mines were exploded along a length of the Messines Ridge. This had a huge physical and psychological effect on the enemy.

The Battle of Passchendaele (also known as the Third Battle of Ypres)

On the 31st July 1917 the British offensive on German forces commenced. The soldiers came out of their trenches and advanced under a creeping barrage which was designed to keep the shelling just ahead of the advancing British troops. The advance quickly faltered, not because of heavy German defences but because of ground conditions and the weather, the worst weather in 75 years. With smashed field drains, the soil quickly turned to mud and the attack stalled. A familiar stalemate situation developed but this time the men lived for weeks on end in flooded trenches and shell holes. It truly was 'Hell on Earth'. It is estimated that the battles of 'Third Ypres' cost the Allies about 300,000 casualties, 35 men for every metre gained. Many of them were lost in the mud of Flanders and have no known grave. They are commemorated on the Menin Gate and Tyne Cot Memorials to the missing.

Mud filled shell holes and trenches

Engineers laying duckboards between water filled shell holes and old trench lines at Passchendaele. This was the terrain across which Charlie had to fight. (NLS).

The record of battles fought by Charlie and the 225th Field Company, of the 39th Division, Royal Engineers, in Flanders

Below is a summary of the 39th Division's battles in the second half of the year 1917. The battles were officially known as 'Third Ypres'. History has recorded them as the mud filled hell called Passchendaele.

In late July 1917, the 39th Division was part of the British 5th Army under General Gough and took part in the following battles known as: **The Battles of Flanders Fields, 31st July – 10th November 1917**.

The following summaries are taken from www.wikipedia.org:

The Battle of Pilckem Ridge, 31st July – 2nd August 1917

'This was the opening attack of the main part of the Third Battle of Ypres. The Allied attack had mixed results; a substantial amount of ground was captured and a large number of casualties inflicted on the German defenders. After several weeks of changeable weather, heavy rainfall began in the afternoon of 31st July and had a serious effect on operations in August, causing more problems for the British who were advancing into the area devastated by artillery fire and which was partly flooded. The battle became controversial, with disputes about the predictability of the August deluges and for its mixed results, which in much British writing were blamed on misunderstandings between General Gough and General Haig and on faulty planning, rather than on the resilience of the German defence.'

The Battle of Langemarck, 16th – 18th August 1917

'A short but very intense second battle fought in very wet weather and deep mud. Huge loss of life was sustained on both sides with no net gain in ground for either side.'

The Battle of the Menin Road, 20th – 25th September 1917

'This battle was the third British general attack of the Third Battle of Ypres. The British reorganised their infantry dispositions, mainly by adopting the "leap-frog" method of advance, which became feasible as more artillery was brought into the salient and by revising their methods of air support of ground operations. Drier weather and extensive road repairs allowed British supplies to be moved more easily. Visibility increased except for frequent ground fogs around dawn, which helped conceal British infantry during the attack.'

The Battle of Polygon Wood, 26th September – 3rd October 1917

'This battle took place in the area from the Menin Road to Polygon Wood and thence north, to the area beyond St. Julien. Much of the woodland had been destroyed by the huge quantity of shell fire from both sides since 16th July and the area had changed hands several times. General Herbert Plumer continued the series of British attacks with limited objectives. The British attacks were led by lines of skirmishers, followed by small infantry columns organised in depth (a formation which had been adopted by the Fifth Army in August). With a vastly increased amount of artillery support, the infantry advanced behind five layers of creeping bombardment. The advance was planned to cover 1,000 –1,500 yards and stop on reverse slopes, which were easy to defend, enclosing ground which gave observation of German reinforcement routes and counter–attack assembly areas. Preparations were then made swiftly to defeat German counter-attacks, by mopping-up and consolidating the captured ground with defences in depth. The attack inflicted a severe blow on the German Fourth Army, causing many losses.'

The Second Battle of Passchendaele, 26th October – 10th November 1917

'A series of fierce engagements took place in the latter half of October and early November. Over one inch of rain fell most days throughout the autumn campaign.'

By the end of 1917 at Passchendaele

By December 1917, the 39th Division engagements were undertaken as part of the British 2nd Army under General Plumer. The conditions under which British soldiers fought at the Battle of Passchendaele were the worst of the entire war, even worse than on the Somme. Cyril Falls wrote in the 'History of the Royal Irish Rifles'- 'The battle will always remain one of the most extraordinary monuments to the courage and endurance of the British Soldier. Those hard-used words are indeed inadequate to describe his virtues. If mortal men could have pulled down reinforced concrete with their naked hands, these men would have done it.'

Cloth Hall Ypres, in ruins. (NLS).

Soldiers returning from trenches in the pouring rain. (NLS).

Below are the detailed entries, in the 225th Field Company Royal Engineers War Diaries for 1917. They include the lead up to the various battles fought at Passchendaele and the actual battles themselves. The first half of the year (January–June) involved less 'fighting' and more 'preparation'. The second half of the year (July–December) involved a series of horrendous battlefield engagements.

Yser Canal	1–10/1/17	The Company worked on Observation Posts at HILLTOP, TURCO FARM, LA BELLE ALLIANCE, LANCAHIRE FARM and HIGHLAND FARM.	
Ypres	11–13/1/17	Major Hammonds returned from course of Instruction. Carried on with work on observation posts. Several Sapper reinforcements arrived.	
	14/1/17	Worked on forward billets in YPRES.	
Ypres	17–18/1/17	Arranged work with 117th Brigade. 100 Infantry reported to Attachment.	
	19/1/17	Work in full swing on MUD LANE trench revetting it and deepening it.	DHH
	20–21/1/17	Worked with 116th Brigade, in assisting men to repair trenches. Also construction of new support line (CAMBRIDGE ROAD) and reserve line (HALF MOON STREET).	
	22/1/17	Started making 16 dugouts in X line.	
	23–29/1/17	Work on digging trenches continued. All work stopped on 29th due to hard ground (frost).	
Ypres	30/1/17	All Work stopped by day on account of bombardment on FRONT LINE.	
	1/2/17	Work on new dugouts and machine gun emplacements continued. 2 mules (light draught) arrived.	

Horses and Mules were used extensively by the Royal Engineers to move equipment and men. (IWM).

Ypres	4/2/17	117th Brigade relieved 116th Brigade in the line. No 2 Section relieved No 1 Section in forward billets.	
	9/2/17	Continued repair to bridges over canal (for second time).	
Ypres	12/2/17	Raid by 116th Brigade on left.	DHH
	13/2/17	Raid by 117th Brigade. Seven sappers from this company went with the raid, with the object of blowing up machine gun posts and dugouts. The sappers were: Sgt. Severs, Sappers Mackie, Richardson, Mellanby, Blair, Wainman and Bradley. Six charges of 25lbs of gun cotton with 8 minute fuses were carried. The raiding party did not get into the German trenches, being held up by machine gun fire. The sappers all reached the German wire. Two of the charges were exploded in it. The others were not exploded on account of injured men nearby. The sappers lay out in 'No Mans Land' until the bombardment ceased and then withdrew without casualties. Sgt. Severs acted with great determination in this affair. Capt. D. H. Hammonds OC, 225th Field Company RE.	DHH
Ypres	15/2/17	3 officers of the 423rd Field Company RE, were shown round trenches for handing over.	DHH
	16/2/17	Company marched to back billets in small parties during the afternoon. Relief complete by 9pm. Horses were tethered in field adjoining back billets for the night.	
Brandhoek	17/2/17	Paraded for marching off at 8am. Extra kit taken by light railway to WORMHOUDT. Marched off at 8.30am arrived LEDRINGHAM at 3.30pm.	
Ledringhem	18/2/17	Day spent cleaning kit, wagons and equipment.	
	19/2/17	Company started programme of training. No football was possible due to muddy nature of ground.	
	20/2/17	Inspection parade at 9am. Ordered to clean cap badges, buttons and equipment. Physical drill and demolition practice.	DHH
Ypres	22/2/17	Party of Officer Commanding, 2 subalterns and 6 NCOs proceeded by motor lorry leaving LEDRINGHAM church at 8am to YPRES to view works of 128th Fld Coy. 23rd Division billeted in post office RUE DE LILLE.	
	22-24/2/17	Company involved with pontoon training. Drill and demolition training.	
	25/2/17	Company marched and entrained at WORMHOUDT for YPRES. All moves completed by 9pm. Company HQ at Post office RUE DE LILLE Ypres and horse lines at OUDERDOM. 100 infantry to be attached.	DHH
Ypres	1-7/3/17	Work continued as normal, digging trenches. 2 Black Watch Officers reported for duty on 6th March. Capt Hammonds handed over command to Capt Argent and proceeded to Division HQ to act for Commander Royal Engineers (CRE) whilst on leave.	

	8/3/17	One officer's charger shot (suffering from tetanus) Pt. W. S. MacDonald 4/5 Black Watch found dead in bed. Work carried on as usual.	
Ypres	9–16/3/17	Re-commenced night work digging trenches and cleaning dugouts.	
	21/3/17	Major Hammonds returned from acting Commander Royal Engineers inoculated.	
	22–23/3/17	Driver Bentham J, wounded by shell fire. Major Hammonds returned to forward billets in YPRES.	
Ypres	27/3/17	3 sapper reinforcements arrived. Work continued as usual.	
	29/3/17	Started work on tramway at VALLEY COTTAGES. Our HQ shelled in the afternoon.	
Ypres	30/3/17	Went round the line starting at 5am. No work done owing to battalion relief.	DHH

Rest Days

Men relaxing on their day off. (NLS).

Ypres	1/4/17	Commanding Officer visited horse lines. Work started on new Battalion HQ owing to shelling at VALLEY COTTAGES.	
	4/4/17	Joined up HALIFAX and ZILLEREKE STREET trenches.	
	5/4/17	Trench work carried on at night. 164754 Sapper Robeson C, and 166432 Sapper Williams N, rejoined Company.	DHH

Charlie Robeson, photographed in April 1917, at Ypres.

Ypres	6–7/4/17	Company marched out to billets at VLAMERTINGHE and then on to WATON arriving at 12.30pm. 1 Light Draught horse died.	DHH
Ypres	8–14/4/17	In camp, undertaken drill, knotting, lashing, musketry training and pontoon bridge building. On the 14th, the Company marched out to YSER CANAL and practised pontoon building.	
	15–20/4/17	Carried on with drill, musketry training and bayonet training. Lecture by Officer Commanding, on discipline.	
Ypres	21–27/4/17	Training on hand bombing and bayoneting. Overhauled explosives. Drill and physical exercises each day. Route march. Cyclists party involved in building new bath houses.	
	28/4/17	Cyclists party continued building bath houses. Remainder of Company all had baths at HERZEELE.	
Ypres	29–30/4/17	Kit inspection, physical drill, church parade. Cyclists party carried out bayonet exercises, bomb throwing and physical drill. Horse inspection for drivers.	

D. H. Hammonds
Major RE, OC 225th Field Company

Church Services

Church services were held regularly. They were particularly poignant just before battle was due to commence. (IWM)

Waton Canal Bank	1–7/5/17	Time spent exercising, cleaning equipment, cleaning wagons, repairing trenches, which consists of joining up gaps in front line. Time spent preparing to dig new forward trench, containing 5 dug-outs in CANAL BANK.	
Ypres	8/5/17	Work interfered with by artillery bombardment.	
	9/5/17	Arranging demolition scheme for Canadian dugouts. Did experimental demolition in afternoon.	DHH
Ypres	11/5/17	Explosives party left trench at 10.30pm covered by a party of 20 infantry from 1/6th Cheshires. Each sapper was accompanied by infantry carrier and one bayonet man. 16 charges each of 4 slabs of gun cotton were carried. 2 adjustable struts were provided for each box to fix the charge against the roof. All successfully exploded. Charges were time graduated 10–15 minutes, from right to left. No hostile parties were met and the party was not disturbed. No casualties.	
Ypres	12/5/17	Belt of wire for new forward trench completed. Other work as normal. Carried on with work on CANAL BANK. Officer Commanding went round the lines in the evening.	
Ypres	14/5/17	FRONT LINE parties cancelled by General Officer Commanding on account of heavy bombardment.	
	15–17/5/17	Carried on with new trench digging. Started work on new observation posts for Royal Artillery.	DHH

There were always new arrivals of men

A constant stream of soldiers moved from reserve to forward positions. (IWM).

Living conditions were a constant challenge

Tommies arriving home at mud terrace. (NLS).

Yser Canal	18/5/17	All available men were involved in digging a new forward trench. 2 Companies of Infantry and 2 of Pioneers were on the work. They completed digging except for a marshy part in centre of line.	DHH
Ypres	19/5/17	Continued new forward trench called BELLINGHAM trench. Started sandbagging.	
	20/5/17	Continued sandbagging with the Pioneers. Finished sand -bagging. Result disappointing.	
Ypres	21/5/17	Continued BELLINGHALM trench. After very hard night, work completed on revetting all but 40 yards. Continued sandbagging. Work on the dugouts continued with infantry only.	DHH
	23/5/17	Rest day owing to battalion relief.	
Ypres	26/5/17	Dug ARMYTAGE trench and revetted 116 yards after cutting through parapet and cutting the wire.	
	27-30/5/17	Spent time repairing trenches. 2 riders,1 pack horse and 3 mules received by Company. Carried on with work as normal.	
Yser Canal	1/6/17	Taped out HORNBY trench. Tape was laid out by officers of the 14th Hants. Some trouble from a sniper on right portion of line.	
	2/6/17	Continued digging out HORNBY trench (3ft wide and 2 ft deep) Considerable trouble with sniper on the right.	DHH

The effect of a mine exploding

In June, 19 massive mines were set off along the British Front Line at Messines Ridge, ahead of the British Offensive. (IWM).

A regular supply of postcards and letters from home reached Charlie, throughout the summer of 1917

Postcard of Stichill Linn. Charlie loved to walk by the Eden Water. Winnie would remind him of it.

(Authors collection)

Postcard of Teviot Bridge. Charlie fished the River Teviot regularly before the war.

(Authors collection)

	3/6/17	Support line (North of TURCO FARM) dug by 14th Hants. Some casualties from shell fire. Started divisional camouflage scheme.	
Ypres	4–11/6/17	Continued work on trenches. Camouflaged observation posts. Front line work delayed by very heavy shell fire.	DHH
	12/16/17	Lt. Halliday killed by shell fire at 2am.	
	14–15/6/17	All work going very well. Heavy shell fire at bridge and damage to bridge delayed material going up. Bridge repairs completed. Wagons came up in daylight with material.	
Ypres	16–19/6/17	Carried on digging new trenches. RAILWAY COTTAGE DUMP heavily shelled. 3 attached infantrymen evacuated, 1 wounded and 2 suffering the effects of shell fire.	
	20–28/6/17	Received orders to move camp. Time spent constructing new camp at ESSEX FARM ROAD. Worked on huts for arrival of 227th Field Company RE near BRIELEN -YPRES ROAD.	
Ypres	1–6/7/17	Work carried on constructing camp. Major Hammonds returned to camp from Commander Royal Engineers office. Work on new divisional camp pushed on owing to shelling of old camp.	
Ypres	7–14/7/17	Work completed on camp construction.	
	15/7/17	Company marched into CANAL BANK to recommence work on trenches.	
	16/7/17	All sections started work at 4.00am and consisted of constructing dugouts, slits for bombs, sidings for tramways, maintenance of screens and construction of divisional dump.	
Ypres	17/7/17	Night parties were prevented from doing much work by heavy shelling with a quantity of gas shells. Early morning parties did well. Very quiet between 4.00am and 9.00am. CANAL BANK billets shelled at 2.00pm. 2 light casualties. Officer's cook house damaged. 7 sapper reinforcements.	
Ypres	19/7/17	Gas attack again all night. Work continued well.	
	21/7/17	Noisy night with heavy shelling.	
	22/7/17	Went round line in morning. Very bad night for gas shelling and other shelling. Respirators were worn from 11.00pm to 3.00am.	
Ypres	23/7/17	Commanding Officer visited horse lines and saw raiding party practising. Pt MacDonald gassed. 1 Private in infantry gassed.	
	24/7/17	Heavy shelling at right of CANAL BANK and forward areas.	

British soldiers on the attack

Infantry going forward on attack to take enemy positions. (NLS).

Below is a record of a raiding party into German Front Line trenches in which Charlie Robeson took part. Eight German prisoners were captured.

Canal Bank Ypres	25/7/17	A Royal Engineers (RE) party of 10 other ranks (OR) accompanied a raiding party of 9th Sherwood Foresters (11th Division) in a daylight raid. Five 2lb charges of explosives were exploded in German dugout bomb stores. One of the Royal Engineers was slightly wounded and several in the infantry. 8 prisoners were taken. The raid started at 4.30am. Hostile barrage was light. The men who took part were: Lce Cpl Knox, Spr Jones W D, Spr Jones C, Spr Robeson, Spr Turner, Spr Gardner, Spr Walton, Spr Brown and Spr Stott....... 159804 Spr Brown was wounded.

Capt. D. H. Hammonds
OC 225th Field Company RE

Army Form C. 2118.

WAR DIARY
or
INTELLIGENCE SUMMARY.
(Erase heading not required.)

Instructions regarding War Diaries and Intelligence Summaries are contained in F. S. Regs., Part II. and the Staff Manual respectively. Title pages will be prepared in manuscript.

Place	Date	Hour	Summary of Events and Information	Remarks and references to Appendices

The page from the official War Diaries recording the attack of 25th July 1917 in which Charlie took part. Signed by DHH (Major D. H. Hammonds). (National Archives).

Charlie with his Royal Engineer pals

Charlie Robeson (standing left) in 1917- Photographed at Ypres.

More postcards from home during summer 1917

The Abbey at Kelso. (Authors collection)

Railway viaduct over the River Teviot at Roxburgh. (Authors collection)

Charlie seldom made any reference to what the Company had been through, in his letters and postcards home to Kelso.

Ypres	27/7/17	Continued work on track construction. Completed work on HQ. Spr. Frost killed, Spr. McDonald wounded.
	28–29/7/17	Half the attached infantry marched to horse lines. Remainder of Company worked on overland track and then marched to horse lines.
	30/7/17	Company remained at horse lines all day. Marched back to CANAL BANK at 11pm.

British Offensive commences: The Battle of Pilckem Ridge begins

| Canal Bank | 31/7/17 | Arrived at CANAL BANK at 2am. Zero hour for the attack at 3.50am. Company received orders to go to work at 5.45am (after capture of Blue Line). Commanding Officer with one man per Section went first with boards for overland track. Company followed by Sections. All Sections at work on track by 7.00am. |

Company HQ first established at HAMPSHIRE FARM but subsequently shelled out and moved to dugout in old German Front Line. Hourly reports of progress sent to Division.

Track ready for use past German Reserve Line by 12 noon. Pack horse track made passable up to ALBERTA FARM. No orders received, so stopped work at 5pm (after 10hrs). Men dead beat.

Company returned to CANAL BANK. The following casualties were accrued: Pnr. Nicholson J F and Spr. Beeston H, killed. Spr. McDonald W J, Spr. Dwane J P, Spr. Howard G P, Spr. Hopper H, Spr. Bowie J, Spr. Smith F, and Spr. Betallack wounded. Spr. Robson T and Spr. Cumberbatch R wounded at duty. Attached infantry–1 killed, 5 wounded and 2 sick.

D. H. Hammonds Major RE
OC, 225th Fld Coy

The following extract describing the Battle of Pilckem Ridge, 31st July – 2nd August 1917, is taken from 'Passchendaele - The Day by Day Account' by Chris McCarthy. Such extracts give a brief summary of what the fighting was like for the 39th Division throughout the autumn of 1917. Objectives in battle, were often referred to as coloured lines i.e. the blue line or red line etc.

'On 31st July, the 39th Division attacked at 3.50am, zero hour, with two brigades, plus one in support. With the aid of eight tanks, it captured the blue line with little trouble. The 116th Brigade consisted of 11th, 12th and 13th Royal Sussex and the 14th Hampshire Regiment. Aided by two tanks which knocked out a battery of artillery, the 13th Royal Sussex captured St. Julien and took prisoners with 17 officers and 205 other ranks. 117th Brigade attacked with the 16th Sherwood Foresters and the 17th Kings Royal Rifle Corps. The 16th Rifle Brigade and the 17th Sherwood Foresters in support passed through. Using Stokes mortars and Rifle grenades as a local barrage, they rushed and took the three pillboxes at Regina Cross. Alberta, another centre of resistance, also fell. 118th Brigade set out at 8.00am with the 1/6th Cheshires, 1/1st Hertfordshires and 4/5th Black Watch. The 1/1st Cambridgeshires were in support. The Black Watch on the left, advanced with little difficulty through Kitcheners wood and across the Steenbeck. On the right, the Cheshires passed through St. Julien. The Hertfordshires however, were cut down by machine-gun fire. The Brigade advanced on the right as far as Von Tirpitz Farm. However the 55th Division on the right, had not come up and the flank was exposed to enfilade fire. The 118th Brigade suffered from heavy counter – attacks, forcing them to withdraw to St. Julien to the east bank of the Steenbeck. They were then withdrawn to Divisional Reserve and the line from St. Julien to the Culvert, was held by the 116th and the 117th Brigades, where they linked with the 51st Highland Division.'

Copy of a SECRET ORDER given to move the Company (HEADQUARTERS 39th DIVISION RE, Order No 36.)

1. 225th, 227th and 234th Field Company's, 225th Tunnelling Company and 13th Battalion Gloucester on night of 30/31st

2. Starting point- Road junction A.30 D1.9
   Order of march- 225th 11.00pm, 227th 11.03pm, 234th 11.06pm, 255th 11.10pm and 13th Regt 11.15pm
   Route: Flank Road to H.2.c.8.7…BATH ROAD to CANAL BANK

3. On arrival at CANAL BANK, units will clear the line of march at once to avoid blocking units behind them

4. Units will observe the usual hourly halts from 10 minutes to the hour, to the hour

5. Units will send orderly with a watch to Commander Royal Engineer's Office at 7.30pm to get the right time

6. Acknowledge.

Canal Bank	1/8/17	Received orders at 9pm to wire the Black Line. I and 3 Sections doing the actual wiring with the remainder carrying. 10 pack animals also carrying. Some German material found at Vanueile Farm. Result was about 400 yds of wire put out either side of ST JULIEN ROAD. No casualties though, considerable amount of shelling onto road. The mud made progress very difficult and the carriers were exhausted after one trip
	2/8/17	Returned from work at 4am. Rested during day. Heavy rain. DHH
Ypres	3/8/17	Went out to work on duckboard track at 4am. Rained all day. Track almost impassable with mud.
Ypres	4/8/17	Almost 1,000 yards of duckboard track laid. Attached infantry ordered to rejoin their Companies. Heavy rain in morning, clearing up later.

Mud and Rain !

Mile after mile of duckboard track was laid by Royal Engineers throughout the war. (IWM).

This famous photograph sums up, more than any other, what ground conditions at Passchendaele were really like. It was taken at the Battle of Pilckem Ridge. Charlie Robeson fought in this battle. (IWM).

Near Vlamertinghe	7/8/17	Transport joined Company in morning. Received orders to march on 8th August. Cyclists went to work on road repair in forward area.
Ypres	13/8/17	Capt. Argent, Lt. Kingsworth, Lt. Summerscale, Lt. Ditchman and 2 Non Commissioned Officers went up to the line to look at work of 233rd Field Company. Men went to billets in BAILLEUL. Major D. H. Hammonds went on leave.
	14/8/17	Company moved to BOIS CARRE. Dismounted men marched to FLETRE.
Bois Carre	15/8/17	Day spent carrying duckboards to FUSILIER WOOD.
The Battle of Langemarck commences		
	16/8/17	Officer Commanding (OC) went round the line with Brigade Major of 117th Brigade. The 5th Army attack took place this morning in which the artillery co-operated, hence line was rather unsettled.
Ypres	17/8/17	Commanding Officer made reconnaissance of Red Line with Lt. Summerscale. Lt. Summerscale wounded and carried in. 101263 Spr Lee evacuated with shell shock.

A silk postcard sent home to my grandmother in August 1917 from Ypres.

Many men who died at Passchendaele were drowned in mud filled shell holes

A wounded man being carried in from the battlefield. (NLS).

Ypres	18–24/8/17	Carried on with trench work on RED LINE.
	25/8/17	Major D. H. Hammonds rejoined from leave. Lieutenant Summerscale returned from hospital. Major Hammonds took over from Captain Argent.
Ypres	27/8/17	Rest Day. Worked on draining billets. Rained all day.
	28/8/17	Continued work on RESERVE LINE and IMPERIAL AVENUE and wiring.
	30–31/8/17	Started work on laying duck board from RESERVE LINE to FRONT LINE. Started work on new billets at VOORMEZELE.
Bois Carre	1/9/17	Continued work on RESERVE LINE. Weather very bad. Heavy rain and wind.

The weather was as big an enemy as the Germans

The ground quickly turned to mud after weeks of heavy rain. Tanks became bogged down. (IWM).

Due to persistent and heavy rain, moving around the battlefield became impossible except on surfaced roads and tracks. (IWM).

Ypres	2/9/17	Organised billets for No 3 Section, in forward dugouts. The back billets in BOIS CARRE were to be evacuated by 2.00pm.	
Brasserie	3/9/17	No. 3 and No. 4 Section and half attached infantry went to new forward billets. Remainder of Company moved to a field near RIDGE WOOD and erected tarpaulins and bivouacs. Forward section started reconstruction work on forward tracks and former German concrete dugouts.	
Ypres	5/9/17	Moved back sections to new billets east of VOORMEZELE. Horse lines moved to BRASSERIE. Fixed a site for The Royal Army Medical Corps (R.A.M.C) in the SPOIL BANK.	
Voormezele	6/9/17	20 men of the R.A.M.C working party arrived and started work on SPOIL BANK. Instructed concrete dugouts to be cleared.	
Ypres	9/9/17	Commanding Officer went round the line in morning and arranged party for night raid.	
	10/9/17	Party of 4 Sappers (Prettyman, Daniele, Jenkins and Holman) went over with a raiding party of 13th Sussex to destroy 2 German dugouts. The raid was not successful and charges were not placed. The officer in charge of the raid was killed and this may account for the non - success of the raid. Good work on trench board track – 450 yards laid.	DHH
Voormezeele	11/9/17	Duckboard track reached FRONT LINE. HQ billets were shelled incurring following casualties: Spr Bradley killed, Sprs Warde and Huggins, died of wounds, Sprs Addison, Hudd, Jones, Utterson, Granger, Porch, Blair, George and Watson evacuated sick.	
Ypres	16/9/17	Same party of Sappers that went over on 10th went over again this time at 6pm. No dugouts were found but the enemy was encountered in shell holes and bombed by the Sappers throwing their bombs. Started mule boarding the tracks for pack transport.	

The Battle of Menin Road commences

	20/9/17	117th Brigade attacked at dawn. 225th Field Company were in reserve.	
Ypres	21-22/9/17	No. 2 Section went out at dawn to repair duckboard track. Remainder of Company went out at 6pm to wire strong points. All officers went in advance to reconnoitre. Heavy shelling between 6.30pm and 8.30pm delayed everybody. Drivers Walton and Clarke wounded. Sappers Lane and Fisher wounded.	
	23-24/9/17	Took all Sections in pontoon wagons to KNOLL ROAD trench. Very heavy shelling of positions causing considerable difficulty and casualties. Lce. Cpl. Maughan and Spr. Jones, killed. Lce. Cpl. Seaton and Spalding, and Sprs. Wickens, Smart and Snook all gassed – wounded at duty, Sprs. Jones, Graham and Stobbart wounded.	
Ypres	25/9/17	Work as yesterday, clearing dugouts. Little was done owing to heavy shelling. Lce. Cpl. Culross T and Jones T.P wounded, Sprs. Cumberbatch and Hopper missing.	

The following extract describing the Battle of Menin Road 20th – 25th September 1917, is taken from 'Passchendaele – The Day by Day Account' by Chris McCarthy.

'On the 20th September, the 39th Division attacked at 5.40am with one brigade. 117th Brigade assaulted with the 17th Sherwood Foresters, supported by the 16th Sherwood Foresters and the 16th Rifle Brigade. The 17th Kings Royal Rifle Corps (KRRC) were in Reserve. On the right, the Foresters pushed on to the western edge of Bulgar wood, taking a number of Blockhouses on the way to the Red Line. The Rifle Brigade came under fire almost immediately from Blockhouses in the 41st Divisional area. They took two of them and pushed on to take the Red Line. At 7.00am the advance continued. The KRRC cleared dug-outs on the way to taking the Blue Line, while the Foresters came under fire from the north-east. By 7.45am the objective was reached and held. A defensive flank was pushed out by the KRRC to gain touch with the 41st Division. Touch was already gained with the 19th Division. At 6.30pm the 1/6th Cheshires (118th Brigade) established a post beyond the Bassevillebeek. German counter-attacks were made at 5.30pm, 7.00pm and 9.00pm but all were broken up by artillery and small-arms fire.'

The Menin Road at Ypres was the most dreaded and dangerous highway on the Western Front

Hell Fire Corner on the Menin Road had to be taken at speed to avoid enemy fire. German artillery had a constant fix on this position. (IWM).

Injured British soldiers on the Menin Road stream back to the dressing stations, watched by their comrades. Charlie Robeson must have had many narrow escapes on the Menin Road. (IWM).

British Casualties: Burying British dead on the battlefield during WW1. (IWM).

Menin Road Ridge: British Infantry await the order to attack again, whilst stretcher bearers in 'No Man's Land' search the battlefield for injured men. (NLS).

Drowning in the mud

'I died in Hell - They called it Passchendaele'

These are words from a line in a poem written by one of the most famous First World War poets, Siegfried Sassoon. There are many famous war poems by others such as Wilfred Owen and Rupert Brooke. Wilfred Owen was killed one week before the Armistice was declared on 11th November 1918.

Passchendaele – A water filled hell hole

The battlefield became a morass of water-filled shell holes, into which men fell and drowned. (IWM)

There was no cover anywhere for advancing Infantry or Engineers. (IWM).

Ypres in ruins

British Troops moving through Ypres showing the devastation caused by incessant shelling. (NLS).

The Battle of Polygon Wood commences

Ypres	26/9/17	The 116th and 118th Brigades attacked at 5.50am for the Green Line objective near TOWER HAMLETS. The 225th Field Company RE and attached infantry, worked on 'B' trench, particularly on the marshy bottoms of valleys. A barrage opened about 8.30pm after which the night was fairly quiet.

The following extract describing the Battle of Polygon Wood, 26th September – 3rd October 1917, is taken from 'Passchendaele – The Day by Day Account' by Chris McCarthy.

'On 26th September, the 39th Division attacked at 5.50am with two brigades. 118th Brigade attacked with the 1/1st Cambridgeshires and the 4/5th Black Watch. The 1/6th Cheshires Regiment was in support. The assaulting battalions met extremely boggy ground and only 'A' Company of the Cambridgeshires were able to keep up with the barrage. By the time 'C' and 'D' Companies had cleared the western edge of Joist Redoubt, 'A' Company was engaged on the eastern edge. A gap developed between the Cambridgeshires and the Sussex to the left, but this was subsequently filled. All the objects were taken, apart from a large pillbox on the left of the Front. 116th Brigade attacked with the 14th Hampshire Regiment and the 13th Royal Sussex. The 11th and 12th Royal Sussex were in support. The Brigade advanced through Tower Hamlets, took all their objectives and joined the Cambridgeshire Regiment (118th Brigade) who were consolidating the objectives on a line just behind Tower Trench, with a post in the north–western corner of Gheluvelt wood.

On 27th September the 39th Division broke up three German counter attacks with artillery fire. That night the 39th Division was relieved by the 37th Division.'

Unloading ammunition at the Front. (NLS).

Voormezele	28/9/17	The Company moved to near ST JANS CAPPELLE. Transported by road at 2pm. Remainder by lorry starting at 6pm. Attached infantry rejoined their battalions.
St. Jans Cappelle	29/9/17	Inspection parade at 10.00am. Remainder of morning cleaning wagons. Major D. H. Hammonds handed over Company to Capt Newhouse and took over from Commander Royal Engineers (CRE) who went on leave. 2 Sappers arrived as reinforcements.
Ypres	30/9/17	Bathing parade at 9.15am. Church parade at 10.30am. Kit inspection at 11.30am. General parade at 3.00pm. Remainder of the day spent cleaning wagons and equipment.

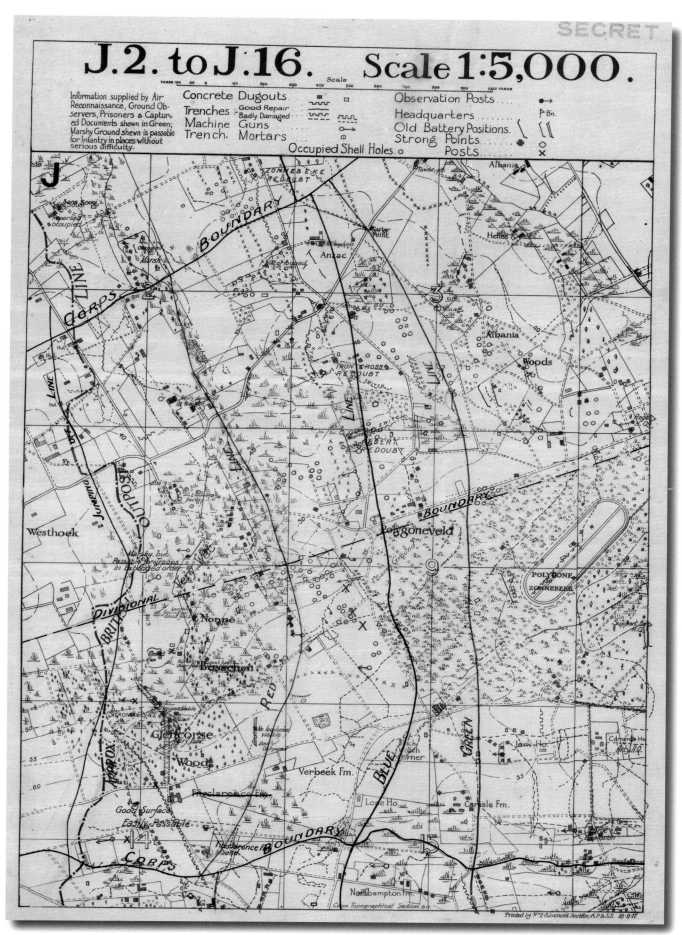

Battlefield Map of Polygon Wood, Passchendaele – September 1917. *Map of Polygon Wood area showing the objectives for Charlie Robeson and the infantry of the 39th Division, the Red, Blue and Green Lines. (National Archives).*

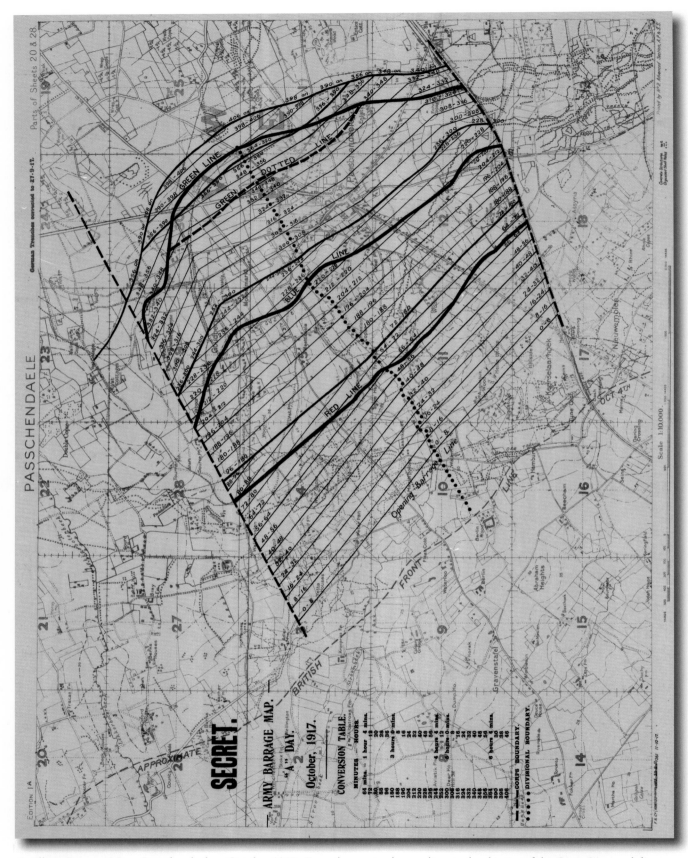

Artillery Barrage Map, Passchendaele – October 1917. *From the opening barrage line, to the objective of the Green Line, each line represented the ground the men of the 39th Division were expected to cover (at 8 minute/100yd intervals) if they were to keep up with the creeping barrage. If they moved too quickly, they would be killed by their own shells, too slowly and the Germans would be in position and slaughter them from their machine gun emplacements. (National Archives).*

British aeroplanes supported advancing British Infantry including the men of 39th Division, near Polygon Wood (September 1917). (IWM).

Infantry defending trenches near Polygon Wood. Charlie and the Engineers of the 225th Field Company dug and then fought from trenches such as these. (NLS).

COPY OF SECRET ORDER OF
39th DIVISION – No 167

The 39th Division will be relieved by one infantry brigade of the 37th Division.

1. The 39th Division will relieve the 41st Division on the Front Line on evening of 22nd/23rd September 1917

2. The 39th Division will extend its position to the left on the evening of the 24th/25th September and be prepared to attack that portion of the GREEN LINE not in our possession

3. After the relief the northern boundary of the 39th Division will be south of RUDKIN HOUSE and BATTERSEA FARM, north of BLAUW POORT and LANGHOF CHATEAU near road junction with SCOTTISH WOOD

4. The 116th and 118th Brigade will relieve the 41st Division Infantry Brigade on the evening of 22nd/23rd September

5. The 41st Divisional Royal Engineer and Pioneer Battalions are placed at the disposal of the 39th Division until 25th September

6. On completion of the reliefs the Brigade Headquarters will be at the following locations – 116th Brigade at CANADA STRRET tunnels and 117th / 118th Brigades at HEDGE STREET tunnels

7. Acknowledge.

St. Jans Cappelle	1/10/17	Inspection of whole Company by Major General Feetham CB General Officer Commanding 39th Division.
Pompier Camp	2-12/10/17	Company moved to new billets. General work on camp construction. More reinforcements arrived.
Ypres	13/10/17	Work carried on at camp. Much rain all day.
	14/10/17	Transported material all day. Lt. Ditchman undertook reconnaissance of SPOIL BANK and LARCH WOOD tunnels for possible accommodation. Conference at 6.00pm to discuss preparations for coming offensive.

ROYAL FLYING CORPS
Reconnoitring the Enemy's Lines.

By the summer of 1917, aeroplanes were used extensively by both sides for taking reconnaissance photographs and for bombing raids.

(Authors collection)

Ypres	15/10/17	POMPIER camp attacked by aeroplane at 7.10pm. 7 bombs dropped (4 in camp and 3 outside). Wrecked 5 Nissan huts,1 cook house, 2 horse standings, 2 newly built hut tracks and fence. Royal Engineer casualties– 4 killed, 24 wounded, 1 wounded at duty, 1 missing. Attached Infantry– 6 killed, 13 wounded, 6 wounded at duty. Pioneers– 2 wounded, Royal Field Artillery – 1 wounded . (Total of 10 killed and 48 wounded) Additional casualties to attached Infantry –12th Sussex - 4 wounded, 13th Sussex- 6 killed, 7 wounded, 1 wounded at duty, 14th Hants- 4 wounded, 5 wounded at duty.
Voormezele	16/10/17	Day spent repairing air raid damage. Buried Royal Engineers killed, at KEMMEL military cemetery. (First 10 places in Row O) Handed over BAROSSA Camp to 152nd Field Company RE of 37th Division.
Ypres	18– 19/10/17	Worked on tracks for Royal Artillery Gunners.
	20/10/17	Moved billets to horse lines on account of persistent shelling in locality. Company now at MIDDLE FARM.
Ypres	22/10/17	Worked on PLUMER DRIVE trench. Very heavy shelling on way up and on the job.

Amongst the slaughter there were acts of compassion.
All men were suffering together.

German soldiers helping a French soldier from a mud filled shell hole. (IWM).

Ypres	25/10/17	No work. Inspection parade at 10.00am. Cleaning wagons and pontoon equipment. Drill parade put off on account of weather.
	26/10/17	18 reinforcements arrived. Men bathed at VIERSTRAATE.
	30/10/17	Started brick standings in horse lines.
Ypres	1-6/11/17	Worked on CANADA CORNER and building Nissen huts as billets.
Canada Street Tunnels	7/11/17	Relieved 227th Field Company at CANADA STREET. Took over maintenance of 'A' Track. Clearing dugouts in BODMIN COPSE. Horse lines remain at location - 0.1.a.0.5.

COPY OF SECRET ORDER NO 46 – HQ 39th DIVISION

1. The 39th Division is extending its left to the REUTEL BREK on the evening of 11th/12th November

2. On completion of the reliefs the MENIN ROAD sector will consist of the TOWER HAMLETS and POLDERHOEKE Sections held by the 116th, 117th and 118th Brigades respectively

3. The accommodation at CANADA STREET tunnels and that occupied by one Company at STIRLING CASTLE tunnels is placed at the disposal of the Commander of Royal Engineers from 12th November for two Field Company's. The third Field Company and 13th Battalion Gloucestershire Regiment will remain at their present location until 16th November

4. The 225th Field Company will move as many men as possible to STIRLING CASTLE tunnels on 12th November

5. Horse lines will not be changed at present

6. Acknowledge.

Ypres	9/11/17	Major Hammonds left for ROUEN to instruct units of U.S Army and handed over command of Company to Lt Newhouse. No 1 Section under Lt Summerscale returned from METEREN. Company carried on with repairing trench board track and clearing dugouts.
Canada Street Tunnels		No. 4 Section was relieved by No. 1 Section and returned to horse lines. Lt. Kingsworth left for course of instruction at 2nd Army Central School. Work continued on sinking well on TOWER HAMLETS ridge.
Ypres	10/11/17	No. 4 Section commenced work on STIRLING CASTLE dugouts for occupation by Company.
Stirling Castle Dugouts	11/11/17	Carried on with extension of track from TOWER to MENIN ROAD. Reinforcements arrived.
	15/11/17	15 Reinforcements arrived. Cpl. E Freeman killed by shellfire.
	16/11/17	The move from CASTLE STREET dugouts to STIRLING CASTLE dugouts complete. Gas shell exploded at head of dugout staircase. Capt. Newhouse (remained at duty) and 10 other ranks wounded and gassed.
Ypres	17-18/11/17	Carried on with work on tracks and dugouts. Capt Newhouse admitted to hospital (result of gassing). Two other ranks wounded by shell fire. Lt. Gillespie left in charge of horse lines and 2nd Lt. McLaughlin in charge of advanced Section.
	23/11/17	No work during daylight. Company concentrated on assisting 227th Field Company with extension of 'E' trench, under Capt. Argent. Vicinity of horse lines at VOORMEZELE bombed at 6.00pm by 2 enemy aeroplanes. About 18 bombs dropped. Nearest bomb landed about 20 yards from driver billets.

A postcard bought by Winnie to send to Charlie during the war.

(Authors collection)

After a year at Passchendaele, thoughts of Scotland and home, would have been uppermost in Charlie's mind

Floors Castle by the River Tweed, Kelso.

(Authors collection)

Roxburgh Castle by the River Teviot, Kelso.

(Authors collection)

Shell shock was commonly experienced by men after heavy shelling

Shell shocked men receiving treatment in a Field Hospital. Men would stare into oblivion for hours at a time. (IWM)

Ypres	24/11/17	The Company moved from STIRLING CASTLE trench to CANAL BANK trench at YPRES. Horse Lines moved from VOORMEZELE to VLAMERTINGHE.
	25/11/17	Parade at 11am. Inspection of clothes and equipment. Company rested remainder of day.
	26/11/17	Major D. H. Hammonds returned from ROUEN.
Ypres	27–30/11/17	Company carried on work on trenches. Vicinity shelled by high velocity guns on 30th November.

**COMMANDER ROYAL ENGINEERS 39TH DIVISION
SECRET ORDER NO 49**

1. HQ of the 227th and 234th Field Company Royal Engineers to move to LUMBRES area and 225th Field Company to BOESCHEPE and COIN PEPDUE. Details of trains will be notified later

2. 225th Field Company (less 1 Section) will be rationed by X Corps school and 1 section will be rationed by X Corps Heavy Artillery

3. The following distances will be maintained on the march- Between Field Companies (dismounted) – 100yds. Between each group of 6 vehicles- 100yds

4. Commander RE in LUMBRES area will be notified later

5. Field Company numbers- 227th -10 officers, 230 other ranks and 70 horses. 234th - 10 Officers, 200 other ranks and 70 horses, 225th - 10 Officers, 163 other ranks and 70 horses

6. Acknowledge.

Canal Bank Ypres	1–2/12/17	No. 1 and No. 2 Sections worked on Transport lines. No. 3 and No. 4 Sections worked on Forward billets.	
	3/12/17	No. 3 section received 'Instructions in wiring'.	
Ypres	4–7/12/17	Continued work on billets and horse lines. No. 1 Section received instructions in rapid wiring.	
	8/12/17	No. 1 Section moved to BERTHEN for work on X Corps Schools.	
	8–21/12/17	Company worked on building new camp schools.	
Ypres	22/12/17	Company received orders to move to VLAMERTINGHE (the main British base and railhead west of Ypres). Dismounted section to move by lorries. Transport and cyclists section by road. Move completed by 4pm.	
	23/12/17	Placed under order of Commander Royal Engineers 32nd Division. Attached to Division for rations.	
	24/12/17	Col. Conchman arrived to take charge of work on wiring ARMY trench	
Ypres	25/12/17	No work today. Only marched to the line, owing to it being Christmas Day.	DHH
	26/12/17	The Company started work on ARMY LINE wiring. Owing to frost and snow, only horses with frost cogs fitted could take to the road.	
Ypres	30/12/17	Moved to forward billets in CALIFORNIA trench.	

Charlie, after the battles of Passchendaele – Christmas 1917

Postcard photograph of Charlie (left) with one of his Royal Engineer pals in December 1917, at Ypres.

Marked on back –

'To Winnie, with love'

Charlie looks in remarkably good shape considering he had spent the entire year of 1917 fighting in Frontline trenches at Passchendaele.

(Charlie's pal remains unknown to us)

The Year 1918 – Return to the Somme and the German Spring Offensive

Early in January 1918, Charlie, the entire 225th Field Company Royal Engineers and the remainder of the 39th Division, were moved from Ypres in Belgium, back to France and back to the Somme, near St. Quentin on the German Frontline - The Hindenburg Line.

The British Army spent the first 3 months of 1918 preparing for a major German counter-offensive. By late March, the Germans were ready. During this time, Charlie's Company was engaged in 'digging-in', building new billets, trenches and bridges for attached infantry battalions, on the former (1916) Somme battlefield.

Summary of 1918

In the Spring of 1918, the Germans launched a massive offensive against the British and the French. This involved the largest artillery engagement of the entire war. All along the Western Front, the Germans had superior manpower, owing to soldiers no longer being required to fight the Russians on the Eastern Front. Although the Germans were numerically the stronger side, the Allies after an initial retreat, managed to halt the German advance and turn things around. By the summer of 1918, the Germans were retreating eastwards, back across France and Belgium. The Allies won major battles at Marne and Amiens and on the 11th November at 11.00am in the Forest of Compiègne, in northern France, an armistice between the Allied forces and Germany was signed and the fighting stopped. The war was over. Other countries involved in the conflict quickly signed peace agreements, but across the world, millions of young men were dead; almost one million of them from the British Empire. Although an armistice was agreed in November 1918, it was not until June 1919 that the Treaty of Versailles was signed between the Allies and Germany, officially ending the 'war to end all wars'.

The War Diaries for January 1918, for the 225th Field Company, records the move from Ypres back to the Somme, back to the bomb cratered landscape they left in late 1916. The Diaries reflect life in the trenches on the Somme on the build up to the German Spring Offensive in March.

British soldiers digging
a gun pit. (NLS)

Ypres	1–3/1/18	The 13th Gloucesters worked with the 225th Field Company on digging new trenches. 100 infantry worked on a tram line.
Ypres	11/1/18	Heavy artillery fire between noon and 3.00pm. Sapper Young killed, Spr. Swales wounded, Lce. Cpl. White and Spr. Wickens wounded – died of wounds.
	14/1/18	Work continued. Capt. Gillespie went to CALAIS on veterinary course.
	16/1/18	Work as usual. Very heavy rain. Drains all flooded.
Ypres	21/1/18	Moved to TUNNELLING CAMP near PROVIN. The Dismounted branch of the Company moved by rail and the Transport branch by road. A lorry was used for spare kit. Move completed by 4.00pm, except for lorry which broke down arriving at 9.00pm.

The 39th Division moves from Ypres back to the Somme, near St. Quentin

Tunnelling Camp	26/1/18	The Company entrained at PROVIN to VAUX SUR SOMME. Detrained at MERRICOURT L' ABBE and marched to VAUX SUR SOMME.
Vaux sur Somme	27–30/1/18	Worked on camp and cleaning wagons and kit. Company moved to HAUTE ALLAINES.
Haute Allaines	31/1/18	Day spent cleaning wagons, inspection of clothes and kit.
Heudicourt	1/2/18	The 39th Division moved into the FRONT LINE, taking over from the 9th Division. Company moved to HEUDICOURT. Attached for work to 116th Infantry Brigade. Daily treatment for trench foot commenced.
St. Quentin on the Somme	2/2/18	Lt. Kingsworth and Lt. Wilson made reconnaissance of work. 100 infantry attached to Company for work. Worked on QUENTIN REDOUBT and SOMME TRENCH. GAUCHE and CHAPPLE TRENCH in very bad condition. Trenches not revetted. Duckboards on average are 1ft below the mud. Front Line strongly wired.
St. Quentin	3/2/18	Worked on deep dugouts for Royal Artillery. Worked on enlarging deep dugouts in QUENTIN REDOUBT and GAUCHE WOOD.
Somme	4–12/2/18	Work continued on CHAPPLE TRENCH.
	13/2/18	Tramway cutting across CHAPPLE HILL trench commenced. 1 Non Commissioned Officer and 3 other ranks attended Anti-Aircraft Lewis Gun course in NOREU.
Somme	14–28/2/18	Worked on YELLOW LINE and REVELLON FARM defences. 5 men wounded and 1 killed on 24th Feb.
	1–12/3/18	Work continued on defences at GAUCHE WOOD and QUENTIN REDOUBT and general improvement of existing trench system.
Haute Allains	12–13/3/18	Company moved to HAUTE ALLAINES and then to FALVY-SUR–SOMME.
Falvy	14–19/3/18	Worked on GREEN LINE trench.

German preparations for the Spring Offensive

'The Germans planned to undertake a massive attack against the British Army during the Spring of 1918. They thought that the British were exhausted, after four major engagements during 1917 at Arras, Messines, Passchendaele and Cambrai. The Germans moved many men and much equipment from the Eastern Front, where they had been fighting the Russians (but were no longer needed) to the Western Front. By March 1918, the Germans were thought to have 177 Divisions in France and Flanders, out of their world-wide total of 241. Of these, 110 were actively stationed along the Front Line. 50 Divisions faced the relatively short British Front Line, on the Somme. 67 other German Divisions were also in Reserve positions behind the Front Line. 31 of these Divisions were facing British positions. This was the best time to strike if the German's were to win the war. It was to be "Der Kaiserschlacht" (The Kaiser's Battle). On the morning of the 21st March 1918, the German offensive began.'

(Source - BBC History)

The Germans' plan of attack for the Spring

The German Commander Ludendorff's aim, for the Spring Offensive (Operation Michael), was to break through the Frontline quickly at strategic points. The main thrust was to be near St. Quentin, where the junction of British and French troops lay. *(This was also where Charlie Robeson and the 39th Division were based)*. They would then head quickly north to the sea, cutting the British lines of communication. The British Army would be surrounded and would surrender. The British Front Line on the Somme in March 1918 was patchy and weak. There were not enough men to defend and hold it and there were no second or third Reserve Lines at all. Ludendorff's plan almost worked.

The actual attack

'Ahead of the German infantry attack on 21st March, a massive artillery barrage sent over 1.7 million shells into the British Lines. The main aim of the barrage was not the men in the Frontline trenches but the military support in Reserve positions. Railway lines, bridges, gun emplacements, food stores, ammunition dumps, roads, vehicles, phone lines and battalion headquarters were all targeted. The intensity of the shelling was designed to throw the British Command into chaos and weaken its ability to organise any meaningful response. It only lasted a short time –a few hours– but it had the desired effect. The German infantry attack was swift and deadly. They quickly overran British positions with their elite stormtroopers. Weaknesses in the British Frontline, were quickly exploited and German infantry poured through. The British Army immediately lost its ability to communicate and began to lose ground. Soon they were in a deadly retreat, fighting hand to hand, across the 40 miles of ground they had gained (at such high cost in lives) on the Somme in the autumn of 1916. Losses would prove more devastating than in 1916, on both sides.'

(Source - The Long Long Trail)

The German Spring Offensive of 1918

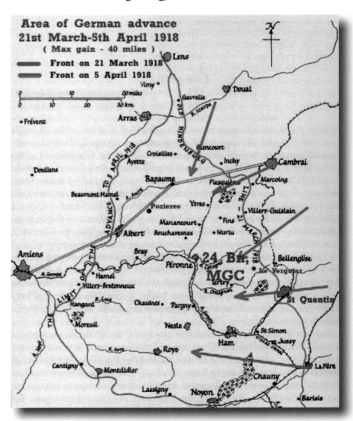

Map showing the focus of the massive German Spring Offensive of March 1918. Charlie and the 39th Division were stationed near St. Quentin on the eve of battle. Between 20th and 30th March they were all but wiped out. (www.kinnethmont.co.uk)

The Battles of the Somme – 1918

Charlie faced his biggest challenge of the war: The Spring Offensive

In March of 1918, the 225th Field Company with the rest of 39th Division were stationed near St. Quentin, 30 miles east of Amiens and were involved in the following engagements from 21st March – 4th July 1918. They were part of the British 5th Army, under the command of General Gough.

The Battle of St. Quentin, 21st – 23rd March 1918.

The Actions at the Somme crossings, 24th – 25th March 1918.

The Battle of Rosieres, 26th – 27th March 1918.

Battle casualties

'Over the two week period between 21st March and 5th April; 177,000 British soldiers are recorded as killed, wounded or missing in battle. Accurate figures are difficult to determine but approximately 15,000 died, 90,000 were missing or taken prisoner and 72,000 wounded. Because the German advance had been so rapid, many of the dead have no known graves.

The greatest losses were to 36th (Ulster) Division (7,310), 16th (Irish) Division (7,149) and 66th (2nd East Lancashire) Division (7,023). All three formations were effectively destroyed and had to be taken out of the order of battle in order to be rebuilt. Six other Divisions each lost more than 5,000 men.

German casualties, for a slightly different period of 21st March to 30th April (which includes the Battles of the Lys in Belgium) are given as 348,300. A comparable Allied total over this longer period would be French losses of 92,000 plus British of 236,300, making just over 328,000.'

(Source - The Long Long Trail)

The Battles of the Lys, 9th-29th April 1918

By mid April, the 39th Division was under the command of General Plumer (General Gough having been relieved, due to the fallback of the British Front Line) and were sent briefly back to Flanders in Belgium where the Division fought in the following engagements:

The First Battle of Kemmel, 17th – 19th April 1918.

The Second Battle of Kemmel, 22th – 26th April 1918.

The Battle of Scherpenberg, 29th April 1918.

Germans moving heavy guns into position during the war. (IWM).

A description of the battles of the Spring Offensive

The long awaited German Offensive started with a massive artillery bombardment on the morning of 21st March 1918. The noise from 7,000 heavy German guns could be heard in London. The British Army was in retreat. In a letter to his men, Field Marshal Douglas Haig said, *'The British Army must, at all costs, halt the German advance'*.

An extraordinary episode now unfolds for Charlie Robeson. On the 20th March, Charlie's Company was based closest to the main launch point of the German offensive, on the Hindenburg Line at St. Quentin. The entries in the War Diary shows the pace and ferocity of the German attack. The Diary entries give a feel for the day on day, street by street, hand-to-hand fighting that took place. The rapid German advance of 38 miles was finally halted after 14 days, on the outskirts of Amiens.

The following War Diary entries, cover the 10 days from 21st March to 31st March 1918 and give details of the final phase of fighting for Charlie and the 225th Field Company Royal Engineers during WW1. Entries are brief owing to the desperate situation they were facing.

	20/3/18	**The MASSIVE GERMAN SPRING OFFENSIVE COMMENCES** **The Battle of St. Quentin begins**
Haute Allaines	21/3/18	The 225th Field Company moved immediately to Haute Allaines.
	22/3/18	A Switch trench was dug in the vicinity of BUSSO.
Clery	23/3/18	The Company moved to CLERY. All wagons, less 4 tool carts were lost to the enemy. Strong points constructed on the west bank of the Somme.
		The Actions at the Somme Crossings
Dompierre	24/3/18	Company moved to DOMPIERRE. Company worked on trenches at HERBECOURT. 2 bridges over the River Somme were demolished.
	25/3/18	The Company held a trench to the rear of HERBECOURT and worked on the defences of the village.
Somme		**The Battle of Rosieres commences**
Cappy, Proyart & Morcourt	26/3/18	4.00am. – Marched to CAPPY, 9.00am - Marched to PROYART. Worked on defences west of the village and held the line for 3 hours under heavy shell fire. 12 noon - Transport moved to CERISSY and forward to MORCOURT. 6pm - Company withdrew to MORCOURT.
La Motte en San near Amiens	27/3/18	Company worked on defences east of MORCOURT and held the line. Held defences until 3.00am – BAYONVILLERS patrolled. Enemy found in occupation of the wood north of the village. Transport withdrew to LA Motte. Lt. Wilson wounded at duty. Company Sergeant Major and 2 other ranks wounded.
Gentelles	28/3/18	Company worked on and held defences of BAYONVILLERS until 9.00am. Transport moved to CACHY and then to GENTELLLES.
	29/3/18	Company holding the line SE of LA MOTTE- EN -SANTERRE
	30/3/18	The Company made 2 counter-attacks at MARCELLEAVE. Major D. H. Hammonds DSO, MC, RE, killed. Lt. McLaughlin wounded, 2 other ranks killed, 17 other ranks wounded and missing. Company withdrawn from Frontline duties.
Bovelles	31/3/18	Company moved to BOVELLES, well away from the Frontline.

The Stormtroopers break through but are finally halted, east of Amiens

Elite German Stormtroopers overran British positions in the last week of March 1918, in a last ditch attempt to defeat the British. (IWM).

A British Machine Gun unit holding their ground in the Spring Offensive of 1918. British soldiers managed to stop the German advance after 10 days of battle, during which time some of the most ferocious fighting experienced on the Western Front took place. (IWM).

A description of the frantic fighting by Charlie's Division, in March 1918

The scant entries in the War Diary shows the tremendous strain the 225th Field Company was under during late March. Over the 10 day period the Company withdrew (retreated) from St. Quentin to Amiens, fighting constantly from village to village, losing men and equipment as they went. Major D. H. Hammonds, the Commanding Officer of the 225th Field Company Royal Engineers was killed on 30th March 1918. (This is a very poignant episode, as it was Major Hammonds who wrote the War Diary entries). The Germans were finally halted 5 miles east of Amiens by soldiers of the British Army, by soldiers including Charlie. As it turned out, this would be the turning point in the war. In their rapid advance, the Germans had sustained huge losses and their supply lines were overstretched. They too were worn out. So much so, the Allies gained the upper hand throughout the remainder of 1918.

Below are extracts from an official report of the activities of the 14 day Spring Offensive. This time period is covered in a letter which Charlie Robeson began writing on 20th March 1918 (see later).

Day 1: 21st March. German bombardment of British positions started at 4.40am, concentrating on positions south west of St. Quentin but extending along a 40 mile front. Trench mortars, chlorine gas, mustard gas and smoke canisters were sent into forward positions. German artillery bombardment target British supply and transport lines. Over 1.7 million shells sent over in 5 hours. Thick mist at dawn (visibility 10 yards) coupled with dense smoke. Although an attack was expected, the ferocity of the attack was devastating. Owing to dense fog which lasted all morning, the German Stormtroopers made rapid advances through British Lines. Most of the Frontlines fell by mid- day. By the day's end, the Germans had broken through the First and Second lines along a quarter of the attack front.

Day 2: 22nd March. British troops, including Charlie, fought frantically, to keep the Germans at bay whilst they themselves were falling back.

Day 3: 23rd March. All lines of defence had now been overcome and there were very few British soldiers left to stop the German advance. Bitter fighting over open country ensued. There was no chance of rest. Despite the dire nature of the British situation, small pockets of soldiers were making a real difference in disrupting the German advance. The fighting retreat of the British 5th Army and the staunch resistance of the 3rd Army were paying off. The German infantry had incurred very heavy casualties and were now beginning to show the first signs of battle weariness. They were starting to extend their lines of supply and were outdistancing their heavy artillery support. All the 39th Division's wagons were lost to the enemy this day. Charlie lost all his personal equipment including his writing case (and makes reference to this in his letter home – see later)

Day 4: 24th March. British troops now fighting in small groups of mixed up Divisions and Units. Phased withdrawal continued in all areas and by nightfall the British had lost the line of the Somme; all the ground so doggedly taken during the 1916 Somme offensive. However, the German line was also beginning to falter. German soldiers were now bogged down in exposed positions on the former 1916 battlefield but they had overrun British supply dumps. All Charlie's Division's supplies were now in German hands. During the day, Charlie and the 225th Field Company Royal Engineers destroyed bridges and river crossing positions to slow the German advance. Charlie spent the evening digging defensive trenches.

Day 5: 25th March. There was complete confusion within British positions. Men were exhausted. No food or ammunition. Units were constantly taking new positions, defending them, then ordered to retire. German troop movement picked up pace and began again to overrun British fighting units. Troops and civilians blocked roadways heading west. The Royal Flying Corps flew many low level sorties dropping bombs on German positions. The village of Herbecourt was defended by Charlie's Company. To the north of where Charlie was fighting, the town of Peronne was abandoned to the Germans.

Day 6: 26th March. Allied Generals meet. French Commander General Foch given overall command of all Allied troops. Orders given to hold Amiens at all cost. German General Ludendorff gave his troops fresh orders to capture Amiens. Frantic fighting all day by the Infantry and the Engineers. Charlie and his Company moved quickly from village to village, fighting pitched battles and skirmishes with hardened units of German stormtroopers.

Day 7: 27th March. A little to the northwest of where Charlie was fighting, the town of Albert was overrun by Germans. Stubborn fighting by members of the 5th Army continued unabated. The 39th Division was fighting running battles all day. Charlie was fighting German soldiers near the village and woods of Bayonvillers.

Day 8: 28th March. Pitched battles all night and all day. The German Army had now advanced 40 miles in 8 days. General Rawlinson replaced General Gough as Commander of British 5th Army. (Gough's replacement was probably unjustified as he and his men had acquitted themselves very well in the face of overwhelming odds. The British Line had been spread far too thinly when they took over from the demoralised and exhausted French Army.) Hand-to-hand fighting continued all day and night for Charlie's Company. Despite great odds, the British Line held and the Germans were halted. Charlie, along with thousands of remaining soldiers, refused to give in. By now (day 8) nearly 177,000 British soldiers had been killed, wounded or taken prisoner in the swift German advance.

Day 9: 29th March. The British fought a thirty-eight mile rearguard action, contesting every village, field and yard, with no reserves and no strongly defended line to its rear. There were 80 German Divisions against 15 British Divisions. The Fifth Army had fought the Somme offensive to a standstill on the Ancre, not retreating beyond Villers-Bretonneux. Charlie's Company was holding out near La Motte-En-Santerre, 5 miles east of Amiens.

Day 10: 30th March. One of the last great German attacks came on the 30th March but the Germans too had suffered massive casualties. The 225th Field Company Royal Engineers came under attack once more near Aubercourt. On that day, a German sniper killed Major Hammonds, the officer commanding Charlie's Company. Charlie Robeson won the Military Medal this day, for 'Bravery in the Field', for eliminating the German sniper who killed his Company Commander.

Day 14: 4th April. The Germans try one final push for Amiens. Tanks were used by both sides simultaneously for the first time. The line was held by British and Commonwealth troops. Fighting eventually relents.

Day 15: 5th April. General Ludendorff calls a halt to the German Offensive. Amiens is still safely in Allied hands. German troops are now pushed back east by British and Commonwealth forces. Charlie's Division is exhausted and all but wiped out. My grandfather and what little was left of the 39th Division is withdrawn from fighting in the Frontline.

Charlie's letter home during the Spring Offensive of 1918

The following letter is a remarkable piece of social history. It was written over the same two week period of the Spring Offensive described above (March 20th – 4th April 1918) by my grandfather to my grandmother back home in Kelso. The letter was started, in the Frontline trenches, on the morning before the start of the massive German Offensive; Thursday 20th March 1918. It covers the 15 days the British Army was pushed back 40 miles from St. Quentin to the outskirts of Amiens, where the German advance faltered and was stopped. It is an unusual letter in many ways (and this may be why it survives), not just because of the description of the battle conditions but because two bullet holes are evident in the paper.

The letter was posted in a green envelope. Green envelopes contained letters home that were not opened or read by censors. They were given to men as a reward for good conduct. Most letters home were read and censored by junior officers, so as not to give away vital information. The letter sheds light on what Charlie and his fighting colleagues were actually experiencing. The letter says just enough to tell that the experience must have been truly horrendous.

Although by now Charlie had spent almost 2 years on the Frontline and had survived 5 months on the Somme in 1916, 12 months at Passchendaele in 1917 and a further 3 months back on the Somme in 1918, it was this battle, the Spring Offensive of 1918, which very nearly cost him his life.

This battle was no heroic pageant as depicted in postcards of the time. This was total war; brutality at its most horrific.

(Authors collection)

For the 14 days following March 20th 1918, over 177,000 young British soldiers were killed, wounded or taken prisoner, in the largest single attack the Germans ever mounted in WW1. Charlie's Division was virtually wiped out.

179

Charlie's letter home to Winnie explaining his situation on the battlefield

Thursday 20th March 1918.

'Somewhere in France'.
(Near St. Quentin, east of Amiens)

"My Dearest Winnie"

Since last I wrote you, I have managed to become the possessor of that most coveted article in the correspondence of the ordinary 'Tommy'…. "A Green Envelope". I think I promised I would write a long letter when next I got one but I did not think I should have such luck to get one, while attached to this 'lot' (Machine gun unit). *However, I have managed it and with a bit of luck, I might get another. Well Winnie, I can't imagine what I am going to put in the letter to make it a long one but it's wonderful what one can get to write about, if there's no chance of it being censored. Of course, we have to be awfully careful because you never know when they are going to have a look at yours. I somehow think that the address has a lot to do with the opening of them. I don't think they will trouble much with ours. However, I am not going to give them much of a chance. We are still at the same place but the weather has broken down completely. We had a lot of rain yesterday and today it is a thick fog - 'Scotch Mist'. There is a terrible row up the road this morning. It woke me up early on and it is now 11am and it has never ceased. I suppose "it"* (the German offensive) *has started but I will doubtless learn all about it in the papers. We have been preparing to move and meantime sitting awaiting orders. I don't know where we will go to or even if we will go. But 'Stand to', is the order. I hope they give him a doing and that we are not needed. I hardly think "we" will move, seeing as we are on this Machine Gun course. Probably we will be sent back to the Company and no doubt they are preparing to move also. I don't know if I will get this posted for a day or two now. Anyhow, if I don't I'll keep on jotting a few things down. No doubt you will be waiting for a line…. So am I. I have got no letters since I came here. I expect the Company will send them on if there are any. I wish this job would last for the duration. We get pretty good food with the R.79 machine gun unit. I have a pretty good place to sleep in and the hours are 9-1. We stop on Sat at 12 noon and don't start until Monday at 9.30. Of course there is nothing to be seen about the place, but we can walk into* (an unnamed town) *in about one hour. There is very little there but it is worth having a look around. I often wish I could have you with me, just to see the ruins as they have been left by the "Huns". It's terrible the damage he has done before he left. I hope* the day will come when they will be able to make him pay for every penny worth of damage he has done. I often think they will run excursions to France & Belgium, just to let people see the state of things. It would no doubt be a paying concern, as a lot of people would be anxious to see the Battle Fields. I myself have seen enough. Well Winnie, it is now 1 o'clock and the chances are we won't move. I hear good reports but I've no proof so far. At any rate, they are going at it for all they are worth. We have to start our lectures at 2 o'clock again, so I will have to have another go after tea. It has turned out a lovely day now and the mist is lifting lovely. I daresay there will be some dirty work in the air in a few minutes. I am beginning to wish my leave was coming on again because it's no good wishing the war was finished. Well, I'm going to have a read at the Glasgow papers before we start. One of the boys has had one sent to him. I'll finish the Epistle sometime tonight if all goes well...........................

5pm. (Same day, 20th March). Well Winnie, I have got the afternoon's instruction over and also had Tea, which consisted of 1 slice of bread and butter. However, I managed to get some biscuits from a canteen not far off. Our Division has gone off and we are left here on our own. I don't know where we are going to get our rations from now but I expect the Officer that is instructing us will see to it. I expect my Company will be going in tonight, worst luck. But I've an idea that we will be on this job for another 8 or 9 days yet. There are a lot of things to learn about a Machine Gun and you have to know every part about it and how to put it right if anything goes wrong..." I can see me murdering some Huns when I go back in the line". I hope you can follow this letter Winnie because I have stopped it so often, that I hardly know where I am about....

It is now Friday morning (21st March) and we have just had breakfast. I would have finished it last night but our 'Corporal' had been out and seen one of the cyclists in our Company and he told him that the Company had come up yesterday and was lying on our left. It was a good walk to them but I set off to see if there was any mail for me. I got a letter and a postcard. Thanks for the letter and I will have to thank 'Flo' for the postcard. It was late on when I got back. All the boys were in bed, so I never got started on the letter. However, I will finish it today but when I'm going to post it I don't know. I might get it over to my own Company if they don't go up into the 'Doings' today. It is just as bad this morning up the road. I expect the 'Counter' is coming off now. Its awful and all for a bit of 'Godforsaken ground'. I can't get to know any truthful details of it. But I've heard any amount of 'yarns'. It is even worse out here for news than what it is in Blighty. But I know that we did not get it all our own way. I hope they get it over soon....

The letter stops abruptly and starts up again 13 days later on Thursday 4th April 1918.

My Dear Winnie,

It must be a long time since you received a few lines from me. I'm awfully sorry, I've never got a chance to send you a line during these last few days. But I'm glad to be able to write a few now. You will see by this paper how near a shave I've had to getting one in the chest. I was recalled from the Machine Gun Company and went into the line with the Infantry. We have lost all our packs and Fritz no doubt has got all my stuff. I was sorry he got Lille's writing case she gave me. I happened to put the letter I was writing inside this book and I pushed it into my Gas Helmet. We always carry them at the Alert position when in the line. That is, in front of you and well up on the chest. We have had days of it and just before we got relieved, we had two bayonette charges against some Machine Guns. This bullet went through the books and glanced along my chest grazing the skin. I must have an awful tough skin; Eh? Well Winnie, I never was in such a do before. We had to keep going back all the time and we could get no food up and as for sleep, it was out of the question. You've never seen such a lot of scarecrows in all your life. Wet to the skin and chats (lice) all over. I wish you could see us. We went into all the houses around and got clean changes of clothes. But the worst of it was, they were all women's clothing. For a shirt, I am wearing a woman's night dress. And there are even funnier things, but that's amongst us. Well we are a long way out of it now; And I believe we are all going to get equipped again. We have lost a lot of men but most of them are only wounded. I'm sorry to say our Major was killed and one of the Sergeants. I hope Fred is all right and that 'Flo' has heard from him. (Fred Haines, was Winnie's sister Flo's fiancé and was killed soon after, in France). I believe Fritz captured the whole Company of Royal Engineers that Alf Knott (a friend) was in but I would not be sure. Now, I will write when I get fixed up but I must tell you, we can only get green envelopes away and field postcards. The officers can't censor any letters, owing to Fritz getting nearly all our transport and they had all the stamps etc on them. Couldn't you steam the next green envelope I send you and send it back inside when next you write? That is, if there are no marks on it. They are awfully bad to get. I have got a few letters from you these last 2 days. Fancy 'Jen' having twins. I did tell her it was going to be a girl but I never dreamt of it being two. I wonder if she knows there is a war on? I hope she gets on all right and that the kiddies are doing well. I will have to write her a line or two. Now I will stop for the present Winnie.

With all my love to you,
I remain,
Yours Aye,
Charlie

The British Army halted the German advance east of Amiens on 30th March 1918. The German Commander Ludendorff's great offensive had been thwarted by men such as Charlie. The hand-to-hand fighting amid the phased withdrawal by the British had taken its toll on the enemy. The 39th Division, however, suffered such a catastrophic loss of men during these engagements (either killed, wounded, missing or taken prisoner) that the Division was withdrawn from Frontline duty. They would never fight in a Frontline position again. This stage turned out to be the turning point in the war. The Germans were steadily pushed back over the coming months and the Allies slowly gained the upper hand until the German surrender in November 1918.

Right are the first and last pages of Charlie's letter home to Winnie in Kelso, written over the 2 week period starting 20th March 1918; the first day of the German Spring Offensive on the Somme.

The letter has a drawing of the Royal Engineers crest, which Charlie drew in pencil. Two bullet holes are clearly seen in the paper.

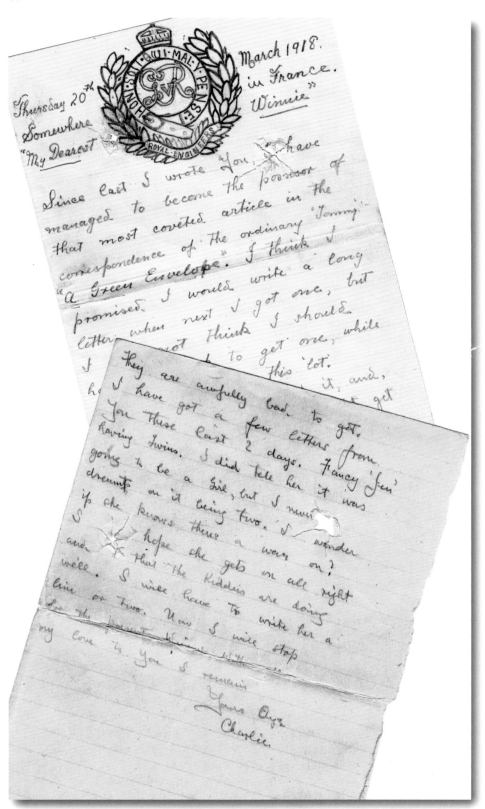

Charlie Robeson won the Military Medal for Bravery in the Field

During the time it took him to write the letter, Charlie Robeson won the Military Medal for Bravery. (The Military Medal was awarded to private soldiers, the Military Cross was awarded to officers.) The following medal award notice shows that it was for *'Gallantry and Devotion to duty north of Aubercourt on 30th March 1918'.* Charlie earned it on the same day his Company Commander (Major D. H. Hammonds) was killed on the Somme. As it turned out, Charlie almost certainly killed the German Sniper that killed Major Hammonds.

Charlie's war medals (the Military Medal in the centre).

The Military Medal.

A Canadian soldier receiving a gallantry medal on the battlefield.
Charlie would have received his Military Medal the same way. (IWM)

Charlie's bravery award notices

Nᵒ 164754 Spr: C. Robeson M.M.
Field Company R.E.

The Major-General Commanding the 39th Division wishes to place on record his appreciation of your

Gallantry and devotion to duty.

North of AUBERCOURT, on March 30ᵗʰ 1918.

Major-General.
Commanding the 39th Division.

Commendation award certificate.

No. 164754 Sapper C Robeson - Official recognition for bravery, signed by General Rawlinson, Commanding Fourth Army, in France.

Headquarters, Fourth Army,

To Nᵒ 164754 Sapper C Robeson,
Royal Engineers

I congratulate you on the gallant act by which you have won the

Military Medal

Rawlinson
Genl.

Commanding Fourth Army.

PRINTED IN FRANCE BY ARMY PRINTING AND STATIONERY SERVICES.   PRESS A

Official recognition for Bravery in the Field

Military Medal Award Certificate. Every soldier who won a medal, had his name printed in the London Gazette. Charlie was 'Gazetted' in September 1918.

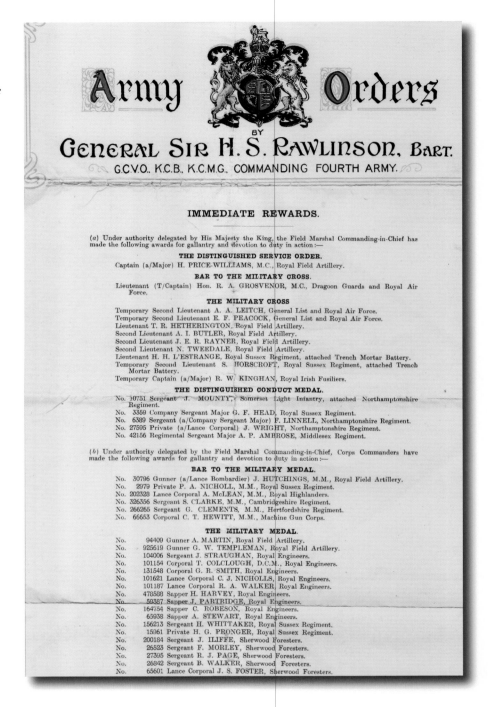

Army Orders
BY
GENERAL SIR H. S. RAWLINSON, BART.
G.C.V.O., K.C.B., K.C.M.G., COMMANDING FOURTH ARMY.

IMMEDIATE REWARDS.

(a) Under authority delegated by His Majesty the King, the Field Marshal Commanding-in-Chief has made the following awards for gallantry and devotion to duty in action:—

THE DISTINGUISHED SERVICE ORDER.
Captain (a/Major) H. PRICE-WILLIAMS, M.C., Royal Field Artillery.

BAR TO THE MILITARY CROSS.
Lieutenant (T/Captain) Hon. R. A. GROSVENOR, M.C., Dragoon Guards and Royal Air Force.

THE MILITARY CROSS
Temporary Second Lieutenant A. A. LEITCH, General List and Royal Air Force.
Temporary Second Lieutenant E. F. PEACOCK, General List and Royal Air Force.
Lieutenant T. R. HETHERINGTON, Royal Field Artillery.
Second Lieutenant A. I. BUTLER, Royal Field Artillery.
Second Lieutenant J. E. R. RAYNER, Royal Field Artillery.
Second Lieutenant N. TWEEDALE, Royal Field Artillery.
Lieutenant H. H. L'ESTRANGE, Royal Sussex Regiment, attached Trench Mortar Battery.
Temporary Second Lieutenant S. HORSCROFT, Royal Sussex Regiment, attached Trench Mortar Battery.
Temporary Captain (a/Major) R. W. KINGHAN, Royal Irish Fusiliers.

THE DISTINGUISHED CONDUCT MEDAL.
No. 10751 Sergeant J. MOUNTY, Somerset Light Infantry, attached Northamptonshire Regiment.
No. 3359 Company Sergeant Major G. F. HEAD, Royal Sussex Regiment.
No. 6389 Sergeant (a/Company Sergeant Major) F. LINNELL, Northamptonshire Regiment.
No. 27595 Private (a/Lance Corporal) J. WRIGHT, Northamptonshire Regiment.
No. 42156 Regimental Sergeant Major A. P. AMBROSE, Middlesex Regiment.

(b) Under authority delegated by the Field Marshal Commanding-in-Chief, Corps Commanders have made the following awards for gallantry and devotion to duty in action:—

BAR TO THE MILITARY MEDAL.
No. 30796 Gunner (a/Lance Bombardier) J. HUTCHINGS, M.M., Royal Field Artillery.
No. 2979 Private P. A. NICHOLL, M.M., Royal Sussex Regiment.
No. 202328 Lance Corporal A. McLEAN, M.M., Royal Highlanders.
No. 326356 Sergeant S. CLARKE, M.M., Cambridgeshire Regiment.
No. 266265 Sergeant G. CLEMENTS, M.M., Hertfordshire Regiment.
No. 66653 Corporal C. T. HEWITT, M.M., Machine Gun Corps.

THE MILITARY MEDAL.
No. 94409 Gunner A. MARTIN, Royal Field Artillery.
No. 925619 Gunner G. W. TEMPLEMAN, Royal Field Artillery.
No. 104006 Sergeant J. STRAUGHAN, Royal Engineers.
No. 101154 Corporal T. COLCLOUGH, D.C.M., Royal Engineers.
No. 131548 Corporal G. R. SMITH, Royal Engineers.
No. 101621 Lance Corporal C. J. NICHOLLS, Royal Engineers.
No. 101187 Lance Corporal R. A. WALKER, Royal Engineers.
No. 478588 Sapper H. HARVEY, Royal Engineers.
No. 59387 Sapper J. PARTRIDGE, Royal Engineers.
No. 164754 Sapper C. ROBESON, Royal Engineers.
No. 65938 Sapper A. STEWART, Royal Engineers.
No. 156213 Sergeant H. WHITTAKER, Royal Sussex Regiment.
No. 15961 Private H. G. PRONGER, Royal Sussex Regiment.
No. 200184 Sergeant J. ILIFFE, Sherwood Foresters.
No. 26523 Sergeant F. MORLEY, Sherwood Foresters.
No. 27395 Sergeant R. J. PAGE, Sherwood Foresters.
No. 26842 Sergeant B. WALKER, Sherwood Foresters.
No. 65601 Lance Corporal J. S. FOSTER, Sherwood Foresters.

Charlie won the Military Medal for the following Actions: *(My father recalled the facts to me which his father had told him).*

On the 30th March 1918, Charlie's Company of Engineers was attacking, with the infantry, over open ground and under heavy enemy fire, near to the village of Aubercourt, on the banks of the Somme, east of Amiens. At a cross roads to the north of the village, a German sniper was targeting British Officers. The advance halted. (War Diary writer and Company Commanding Officer Major Hammonds was probably killed at this point and Lt. McLaughlin wounded). A volunteer was sought, to go and eliminate the German sniper. Charlie volunteered and went out from the Company to locate the German rifleman. He killed the German sniper and took his binoculars (see photo) and also the German's razor, as Charlie had lost all his personal effects, in the hand-to-hand fighting, of the previous 2 weeks.

German snipers were a constant threat to soldiers on the move. (IWM).

Binoculars taken by Charlie from the German sniper

These German snipers binoculars were parcelled up and given to an unknown soldier heading back to England on leave. Charlie asked the soldier to post the parcel to Scotland when he landed back in England… which he did. My grandmother received the binoculars the same week.

Charlie's sister is relieved to hear he is alive

Back home, a couple of weeks later, the following hand written letter from Charlie's sister Anne (who lived at Torwood House, Lilliesleaf) is thanking Winnie for forwarding the letter to her, informing her that her brother was safe.

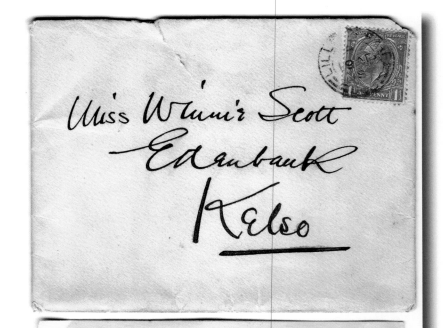

Recuperating soldiers of the Spring Offensive May 1918, at a Military Hospital in Norwich. Charlie is seen here getting fighting fit to go back to the Frontline (standing 5th from right hand side, second back row).

Charlie's letter home from the Base Hospital in Norwich in May 1918

Charlie wrote this letter to Winnie from the Base Hospital in Norwich, where he had been sent to rest after being hit in the chest by rifle fire, during the battles of the Spring Offensive, on the Somme.

The envelope from Charlie is dated Saturday 4th May 1918 (passed by censor 1348, postmarked 7th May 1918)

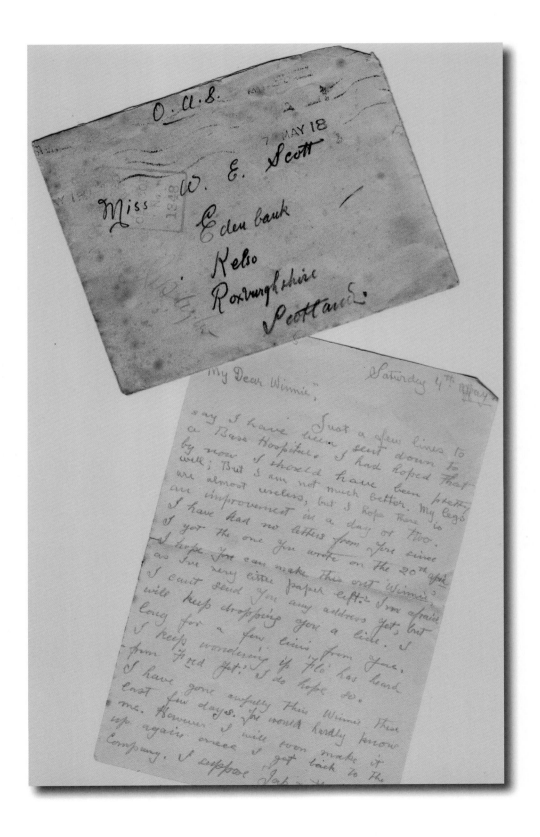

The typed contents of the letter

'My Dear Winnie'

Just a few lines to say that I have been sent down to a Base Hospital. I had hoped that by now I should have been pretty well. But I am not much better. My legs are almost useless but I hope there is an improvement in a day or two. I have had no letter from you since I got the one you wrote on 20th April. I hope you can make this out Winnie, as I have very little paper left. I'm afraid I can't send you any address yet but will keep dropping you a line. I long for a few lines from you. I wonder if Flo has heard from Fred yet. I do hope so. (Fred was, by now, dead). I have gone awfully thin Winnie, the last few days. You would hardly know me. However, I will make it up again, when I get back to the Company. I suppose Jack and the family are still going on all right. I

expect a few more men will be getting called up under this new Act. That is if there is anybody left. Yes, I think Mr Darling will be safe enough as I think he is behind the lines. Of course, 'Fritz' pays special attention to these places, if he gets to know where they are, especially at night with his planes. I see they are on about this Peace Movement again. It's an awful funny war. How I wish it was finished. I wrote to Mother the other day. I expect they will be getting along alright. I haven't heard from them in ages. Well Winnie, I think I will stop for now and I hope this finds you well.

With fondest love

I remain

Yours Aye

Charlie

World War One postcard, in praise of the work of the Royal Engineers. (Authors collection)

Back with the Engineers

Drill and physical exercise were regular activities for recuperating soldiers. (Charlie is up front, pulling the gun carriage, with rope round his right shoulder).

Silk postcards that Charlie sent home from France in 1918

Two silk cards which Charlie picked up in France, show the towns of St. Quentin and Peronne in Flames.

By April 1918, the 225th Field Company Royal Engineers was so heavily depleted of men and so exhausted from 2 years of constant fighting on the Frontline, that it was sent (along with what little remained of the 39th Division) into a Reserve Position, well behind enemy lines. The men were moved to nearer the French coast, to work on transit camps for incoming British troops and also on construction of new camps for the arrival and training of American troops. Because of the trauma they had suffered during 2 long years of fighting, the 225th Field Company never occupied a Frontline position again. Though they didn't know it, the British Army had turned the tide. During the Spring of 1918, the British Army had broken German resolve. From this point on, Britain and her Allies began to win the war.

They will not break through

By the summer of 1918, Charlie and the soldiers of the 39th Division, had the job of defending the Channel ports. (Authors collection)
By now American troops were arriving in large numbers.

The British Army begins the final push to end the war.

'The defeat of Germany's resolve had taken place on the British sector by British soldiers, between March and July 1918. It was the fighting ability and utter determination of the ordinary British soldier that finally won the war.

The Great War had cost the 39th Division 27,869 men killed, wounded or missing.'

(Source- The Long Long Trail)

The War Diaries of the 225th Field Company Royal Engineers, continues into the final phase of the conflict, the training of American troops.

Bovelles	1/4/18	The Company moved to near BOVELLES. Day spent cleaning and checking equipment.
Aumont, Le Fay and Dargnies	2- 4/4/18	The Company moved to AUMONT and LE FAY then DARGNIES and spent the next 4 days overhauling equipment.
Moule	9/4/18	Entrained at WOINCOURT for ST OMER. Marched to MOULLE.

Bayenghem	10/4/18	Moved to BAYENGHEM. No. 3 Section under Lt. Robertson moved to LICQUES and No. 4 Section under Lt. Kingsworth moved to LE POIRIER. Lt. Ditchburn detailed for Gas Course.
	11–18/4/18	Worked on additions and improvements to Rifle Ranges and assault courses for use by the 77th Division US Army shortly expected to arrive.
	18/4/18	Capt. Gillespie and 2nd Lt. Ditchburn and 4 NCOs proceeded to 302nd Regiment USA Engineers, to act as Instructors. 3 x 30 yard rifle ranges completed.
Guemy	19–30/4/18	Continued work on new rifle ranges, erecting 'gas proof huts' and new assault courses. Commenced erecting map shelters at HQ for units of US Army, 77th Division. On 23rd moved to GUEMY.
	1–24/5/18	Continued work on camp for arrival of US Infantry. Days spent constructing rifle ranges, assault courses, building huts, building lecture room, building map rooms at LICQUES, NORDAUSQUES and SANGHEN. Capt Gillespie left for 6 months in England.
	25/5/18	Completed 116th Brigades gas ground, with exception of fixing gas blankets.
Guemy	2/6/18	Continued work on Divisional HQ at WOLPHUS.
	10/6/18	Completed a 500 and 600 yard rifle range at GUEMY.
	13–30/6/18	Completed work for water point at MONNECOVE. Orders received for erection of a dummy village for practice attack.

American troops receive training in trench construction

The 225th Field Company Royal Engineers spent time teaching newly arrived US troops the art of trench warfare.

(Authors collection)

Colembert	1–31/7/18	The Company continued work on camp. Building bath houses, map houses. Moved to COLEMBERT on 19th July. Completed hut for HQ 39th Division at WOLPHUS.

On the Home Front: Women were the unsung heroes of World War One

The Woman's Land Army

In the early part of the twentieth century, Britain imported 70% of the food needed to feed its population. Because Britain is an island nation, imported food had to run a blockade set up by German submarines and ships. Imported food became scarce, so food production at home had to be increased massively. Over 100,000 women joined the Women's Land Army which was set up in 1917 to provide a workforce to run the farms.

Reproduced from "The Sphere." **HELP THE WOUNDED.**

Injured soldiers desperately needed nursing.   (Authors collection)

Keeping the Home Fires Burning

Women at home looked after the children, fed and cooked, washed and cleaned, worked in factories and farms and still had time to write letters to their husbands and sons. Personal letters, cards, food, embroidered handkerchiefs and items of clothing were all parcelled up and sent to France as mementos of home. Psychologically, keeping ties with home meant everything to the soldiers at the Front.

'Up to and including the Edwardian era, a woman's role in the workplace was generally restricted to domestic service, nursing, teaching and agricultural work. Women in factories did menial and repetitive tasks and were paid a small percentage of what their male counterparts earned. The Great War changed the role of women in the work place forever. Women were called upon to take up men's roles in factories, mines and many other work places, where traditionally men carried out the work. Women were the unsung heroes of the war; tending the fields, keeping the industrial wheels turning and the home fires burning.'

(Source – millicentsutherlandambulance.com)

Nursing the injured troops

'When a soldier was injured on the battlefield, depending on the type and extent of his wounds, he would either struggle on his own, be carried by a comrade or placed on a stretcher and taken to the regimental aid post situated somewhere on the edge of the battlefield. Stretcher-bearers, trained in first aid, treated haemorrhages and gave other immediate help. At the aid post, the wound was dressed and then the soldier was taken further back to a field dressing station. After having an anti-tetanus injection, he was sent by ambulance, to a casualty clearing station (CCS) situated well behind the line. When fit enough, he was put on a hospital train which took him to a base hospital. He then either returned to fight again or was sent back to Britain to a military hospital or another centre, where he could convalesce.'

(Source – millicentsutherlandambulance.com)

Back home in Kelso, Winnie was a nurse providing rest and recuperation for injured soldiers

During the war, my grandmother kept herself busy tending injured troops. Although Winnie worked in service at Eden Bank House, she also worked as a nurse at Newton Don House, which along with neighbouring Eden Hall, were used respectively as an Auxiliary Hospital and Military Hospital for recuperating soldiers.

Newton Don House, Kelso 1917. Used as a hospital for injured soldiers during WW1.

This postcard was sent by Sapper R. Hall Royal Engineers, from Newton Don to Stoke-on-Trent, where his uncle lived. It was posted in Kelso on 24th March 1917.

It reads:

Dear Uncle,

I expect you heard about me getting wounded. It was about seven weeks ago. I'm getting on nicely and hope to be seeing you soon. This is a fine place. It belongs to Captain Balfour of the Scots Guards,

Best Love,

Roland.

Auxiliary Hospitals

At the outbreak of the First World War, the British Red Cross and the Order of St. John of Jerusalem combined to form the Joint War Committee. They pooled their resources under the protection of the Red Cross emblem. As the Red Cross had secured buildings, equipment and staff, the organisation was able to set up temporary hospitals as soon as wounded men began to arrive from abroad.

'Auxiliary Hospitals were attached to central Military Hospitals, which looked after patients who remained under military control. There were over 3,000 Auxiliary Hospitals administered by Red Cross county directors. In many cases, women in the local neighbourhood volunteered on a part-time basis. The hospitals often needed to supplement voluntary work with paid roles, such as cooks. Local medics also volunteered, despite the extra strain that the medical profession was already under at that time. The patients at these hospitals were generally less seriously wounded than at other hospitals and they needed to convalesce. The servicemen preferred the auxiliary hospitals to military hospitals because they were not so strict, they were less crowded and the surroundings were more homely.'

(The Red Cross)

Eden Hall was used as an Auxiliary Hospital during WW1.

(Authors collection)

'Eden Hall became a hospital for limbless sailors and soldiers in June 1915 and had beds for 36 men. By November 1918, Eden Hall had become overcrowded and the health board planned to move the men to Pinkieburn Hospital near Musselburgh. From the 3 years (to June 1918), that the hostel operated at Kelso, 987 men were fitted with artificial limbs, including 18 cases of double amputation. This figure did not embody all the maimed soldiers who were fitted with artificial limbs by the Hostel surgeon. The total number of men supplied with artificial limbs at Eden Hall up to 1919 were: Leg cases: 1,176 and arm cases: 405. The admirable service rendered to the nation by the Commandant of the Hostel, Mrs Isobel Douglas Home and Matron Mrs George Henderson, was recognised by the government and each received the honour of being awarded the Royal Red Cross.'

(Eden Hall Hostel Report 1919)

Winnie nursed soldiers during the war

Nursing at Lednathie House, Kirremuir, Forfar c.1916. Winnie, (second from front in nurse's uniform), during WW1 with friends Greta Todd, May Lyall, Mrs Brunton and Minnie Roxburgh.

Nurse Winnie Scott at Eden Bank House Kelso, with 2 recuperating soldiers (Private Thomson and Sergeant Hunter), from Newton Don Auxiliary Hospital, c.1917.

Home support for the war effort

(Alastair Brooks)

Visit of 'Julian the Tank Bank' to Kelso on 10th October 1918. This Mark IV tank was one of 6 war worn tanks that travelled around the country promoting the sale of government war bonds. A tank would arrive with great fanfare and civic dignitaries would greet the tank and speeches would be made from the top of it. The tank would be accompanied by soldiers and artillery guns. Sometimes an aeroplane would drop pamphlets over the town prior to the tank's appearance encouraging people to invest. My grandmother may well have attended and have been in this photograph.

A very early aerial photograph of Kelso c.1918. Possibly taken as part of the war bonds promotional leaflet drop and the visit to the town of the tank bank.

(Authors collection)

Winnie collected memories of her time during the war

*Winnie (on right) with Mrs Dickson and May
Veitch at Eden Bank House. c.1917.*

*Alexander Scott (December 1914) - Winnie's father
volunteered in WW1. He trained at Stobs Camp Hawick.
He was nearly 50 years old.*

*Below is a copy of an autograph book kept by Winnie during WW1
and signed by injured soldiers and friends at Eden Bank, Newton
Don, Lednathie and Kelso. The note book was given to Winnie by
her sister Flo, on the occasion of her birthday in 1915.*

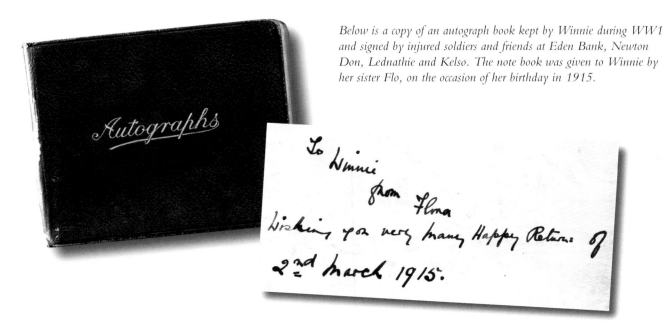

Pages from Winnie's WW1 note book, which injured soldiers signed.

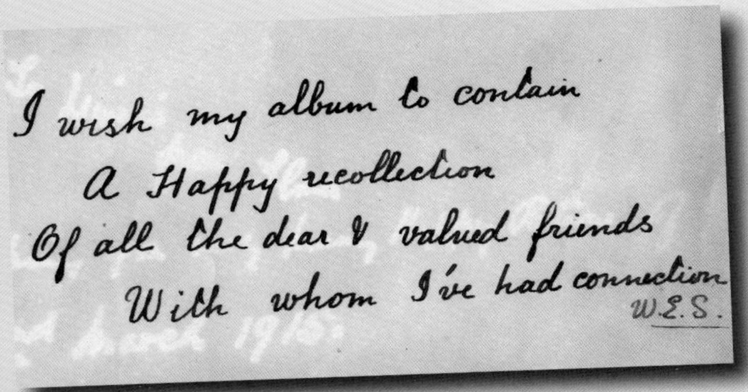

I wish my album to contain
A Happy recollection
Of all the dear & valued friends
With whom I've had connection
W.E.S.

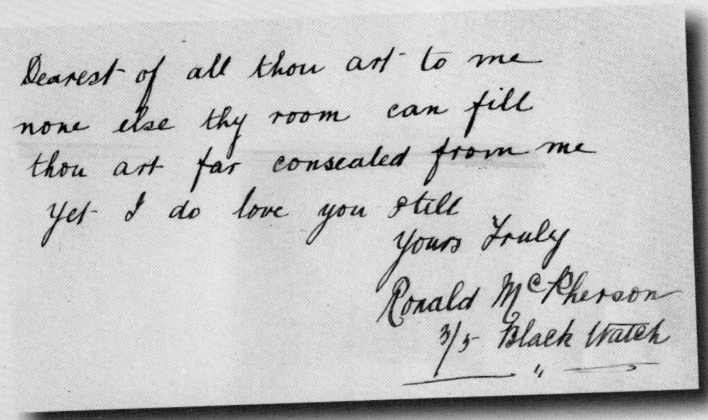

Our hands have met the years begun
Greetings kind we give each other
Prosperous be your outs and ins
Comrade Sweetheart Friend and Brother

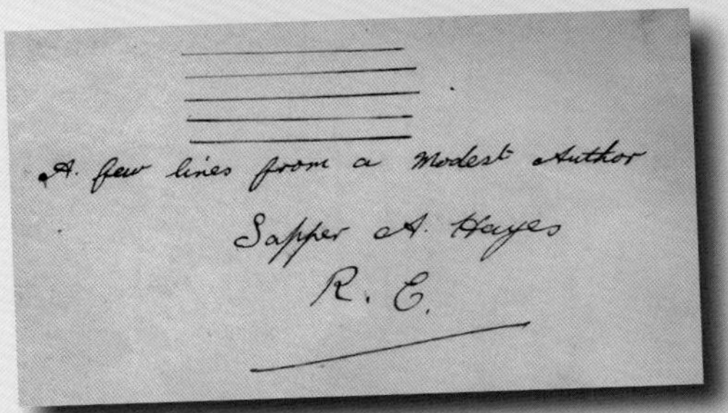

Dearest of all thou art to me
none else thy room can fill
thou art far concealed from me
Yet I do love you still
Yours Truly
Ronald McPherson
3/5 Black Watch

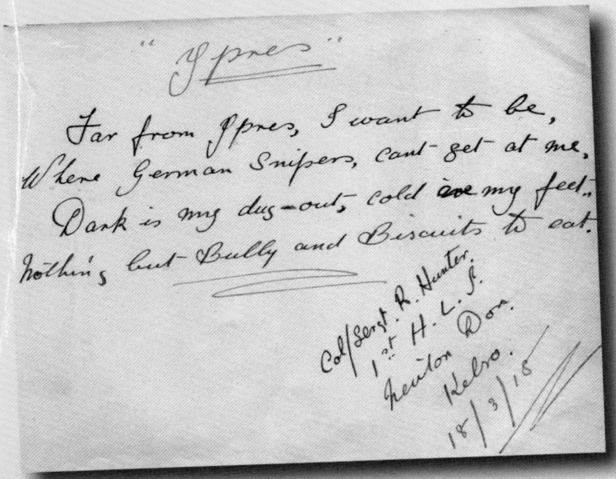

A few lines from a Modest Author
Sapper A. Hayes
R. E.

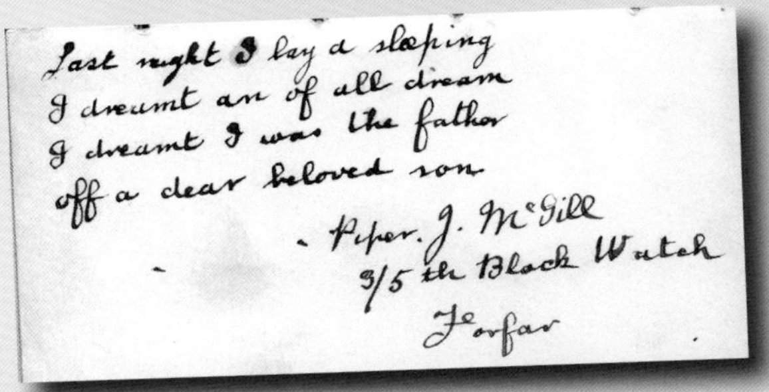

Last night I lay a sleeping
I dreamt an of all dream
I dreamt I was the father
off a dear beloved son
Piper. J. McGill
3/5 th Black Watch
Forfar

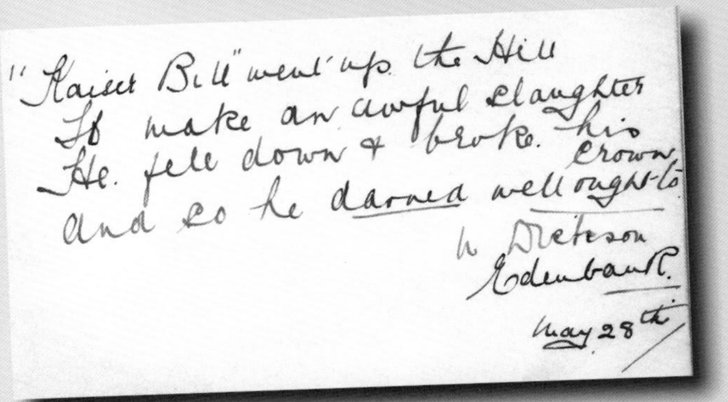

"Ypres"
Far from Ypres, I want to be,
Where German Snipers, can't get at me.
Dark is my dug-out, cold are my feet,
Nothing but Bully and Biscuits to eat.
Col/Serjt R. Hunter,
1st H.L.I.
Newton Dom
Kelso.
18/3/18

"Raive Bill" went up the Hill
To make an awful slaughter
He fell down & broke his Crown
And so he darned well ought to
W Dickeson
Edenbank
May 28th

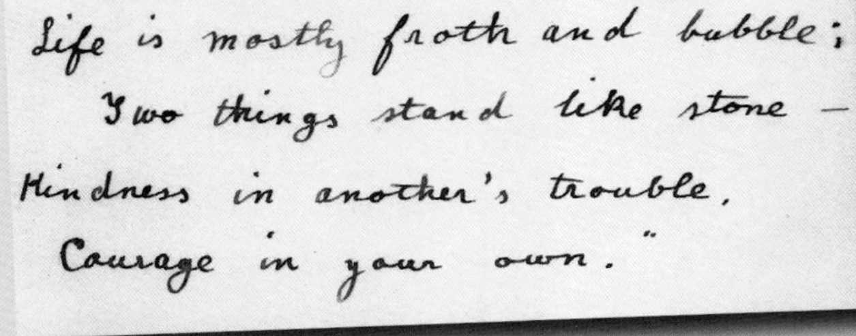

Life is mostly froth and bubble;
Two things stand like stone —
Kindness in another's trouble,
Courage in your own."

*Heartfelt words written by a soldier
in Winnie's autograph book.*

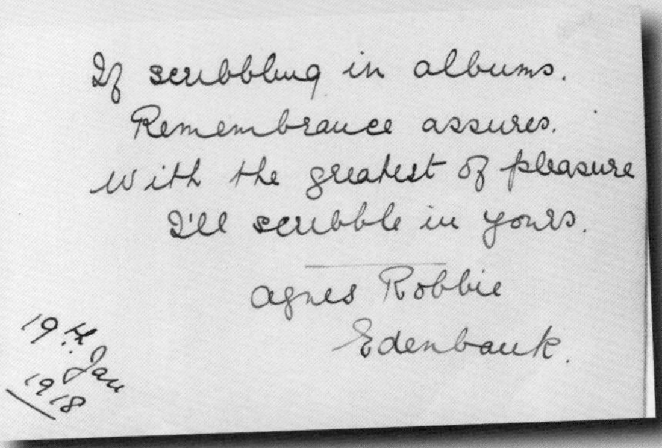

If scribbling in albums.
Remembrance assures.
With the greatest of pleasure
I'll scribble in yours.
Agnes Robbie
Edenbank
19.H.
Jan
1918

The war nears its end and the War Diaries record the final months

	14/8/18	No. 4 Section under Lt. Kingsnorth left by route march for CALAIS. Remainder of Company entrained at NORTKERQUE. No. 1 Section under Lt. Brand for ROUEN. No. 3 Section under Lt. Robertson for LE HAVRE and Headquarters Section for VARENGUEVILLE in DIEPPE area.
Varengueville	16/8/18	Detrained at OUVILLE and marched to billets in VARENGUEVILLE.
	19/8/18	No. 1 Section worked on detention camp at ROUEN. No. 2 Section worked on training camp near COCU. No. 3 Section worked for Commander Royal Engineers at LE HAVRE and No. 4 Section worked for 58th Company RE at CALAIS. All Sections worked on into September.
	1–30/9/18	Continued work on US Infantry training camps throughout September. Building Nissen huts, digging drains, repairing roads, creating horse standings etc.
Verengueville	To–10/10/18	Ongoing work on camp construction. Built parade ground, laid football pitches, built new bath houses, stables and roofing for horse lines. Instructor Officers' huts built.
	To–19/11/18	Work continued on Officers' huts

Your King and Country Thank You.

HOME WORDS No. 168

Christmas Greetings from   to

On 11th November, the Armistice was signed in a railway carriage in woodlands near Compiegne. The war was over.

World War I Propaganda

The war was at an end. This piece of propaganda was kept by Charlie.

THE KAISER'S DESPAIR.

Realising that the end is near he makes his Will.

From our special correspondent in Berlin.

It is rumoured in Germany that the Emperor now realises that his number is up, and is accordingly making his Will, revoking all Wills made heretofore.

The Will is said to read as follows :

This is the last Will and Testament of me WILHELM, the super-swanker and ruler of the sausage-eaters, recognising that I am fairly up against it, and expecting to meet with a violent death at any minute at the hands of brave Johnny Bull, hereby make my last Will and Testament.

I appoint the Emperor of Austria to be my sole executor (by kind permission of the allies).

1. **I give and bequeath** to France the territories of Alsace and Lorraine (as this is only a case of returning stolen property, I don't deserve any credit for it, and am not likely to get it either).

2. **To** Servia I give Austria.

3. **To** Russia I give Turkey, for the Tzar's Christmas Dinner.

4. **To** Belgium I should like to give all the thick ears, black eyes, and broken noses, that she presented me with when I politely trespassed on her territory.

5. **To** Admiral Jellicoe I give all my Dreadnoughts, Submarines, Torpedo-boat destroyers, and fleet of Funkers generally what's left of them. He's bound to have them in the end, so this is only anticipating events.

6. **To** John Bull I give what's left of my Army, as his General French seems so handy at turning my men into sausage-meat, I suppose he means to finish the job with his Kitchener, the champion German-sausage cooker.

7. **To** the British Museum I leave my famous moustaches, souvenir of the greatest swanker in this or any other age.

8. **To** Mrs. Pankhurst and the wild women I leave my mailed fist, they'll find it useful, no doubt, when they resume their Militant tactics.

9. **To** Sir Ernest Shackleton I leave the Pole, I've been up it for so long that I regard it as my own property.

Signed   H.I.M. WILHELM,
German Emperor.
Lord of the Land, Sea, and Air
Not forgetting the Sausages and Lager Beer.

Signed by the above-named WILHELM as his last Will in the presence of us his ministers and keepers present at the same time, who in his presence and in the presence of each other, have hereunto subscribed our names as witnesses.

Baron Von Sauerkraut.
Graf von Munichlagerbier.

Dunkirk	20/11/18	All work held in abeyance at No. 2 Camp, until further orders received, by order of Commander Royal Engineers at LE HAVRE. **(This was probably as a result of the Armistice / Ceasefire called on 11/11/18, signed in a clearing in the Forest of Compiegne, north east of Paris, France)**
	21–25/11/18	Work continued on No. 1 and 4 camps. Work on No. 3 camp stopped by order of Commander Royal Engineers LE HAVRE, ROUEN and CALAIS. Awaiting orders for Company to concentrate in DIEPPE area.
	26–30/11/18	Company ordered to concentrate at ST MARTIN EGLISE (4 miles South East of DIEPPE). Meanwhile Company worked on buildings at Camps 1 and 4.
	1/12/18	Received orders to move Company HQ. All detached staff and Transport to DUNKIRK area.
	2–3/12/18	No. 4 Section entrained at CALAIS under command of Capt. Hutton. Major Day left for England on short leave. Transport to move at 10am on 3rd and personnel at 1300hrs. No. 2 Section entrained at ETAPLES.
	4–7/12/18	All sections now arrived DUNKIRK. All Sections employed erecting huts at MARDYCK Camp – for demobilisation
	9/12/18	Lt. Kingsnorth, Lt. Broomhall and Lt. Ditchburn admitted to hospital with influenza.
	25/12/18	Christmas Day- Rest Day.

A Christmas card from home.

A Christmas card sent to Winnie in December 1918

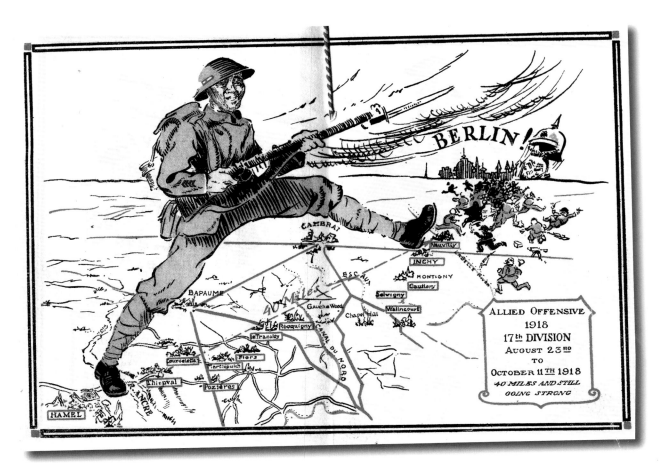

The Christmas card shows the ground gained in the final battles of 1918, which brought the war to an end.

1919 – The end of the war and demobilisation

26–31 12/18	Work continued on camp hutting.	
1–12/1/19	Camp now Brigade HQ for 39th Division. Men being demobilised one at a time or in small groups each day. Capt. Wilson demobilised while on leave in UK.	
13–21/1/19	Lt. Kingsnorth and 2 men demobilised.	
26/1/19	Driver Mace J. M. died of influenza in 8th Canadian Station hospital. Work on huts and demobilisation continues.	
28/1/19	Work on huts and demobilisation continues. 7 Riders, 4 light draught, 4 pack horses and 20 light draught mules demobilised.	
1/2/18–30/6/18	Work and demobilisation as normal	
1–10/7/19	Bridging wagons, stores and remaining equipment sent to BEAUMARIS.	
11/7/19	Transport sent to BEAUMARIS.	
12/7/19	Unit disbanded.	

Major Day, Officer Commanding
225th Field Company Royal Engineers

58730

CERTIFICATE of { Discharge ~~Transfer to Reserve~~ ~~Disembodiment~~ Demobilization } on Demobilization.

Army Form Z. 21.

Regtl. No. 164754. Rank Spr

Names in full Robeson, Charles
(Surname first)

Unit and Regiment or Corps
from which
*Discharged
~~Transferred to Reserve~~ } 178 fld Coy RE

Enlisted on the 24-2-16 Mob 24-4-1916

For Royal Engineers
(Here state Regiment or Corps to which first appointed)

Also served in ....

Only Regiments or Corps in which the Soldier served since August 4th, 1914, are to be stated.
If inapplicable, this space is to be ruled through in ink and initialled.

†Medals and
Decorations
awarded during
present engage-
ment } Awarded Military Medal
vide London Gazette 9/13.9.18

Nil

*Has ~~Has not~~ } served Overseas on Active Service.

Place of Rejoining in
case of emergency } Irvine   Medical Category A.I

Specialist Military
qualifications } Harness Maker   Year of birth 1888

He is* { ~~Discharged~~ ~~Transferred to Army Reserve~~ ~~Disembodied~~ Demobilized } on 2-3-1919

in consequence of **Demobilization.** Lieut
.... " Signature and Rank.

Officer i/c RE Records. Chatham (Place).

* Strike out whichever is inapplicable.   † The word "Nil" to be inserted when necessary.

(20996). Wt. W 8211—P.P. 2329. 3,000m. 1/19 D & S. (E 1256.),

Charlie Robeson was demobilised on 2nd March 1919. This is a copy of his demobilisation papers.

Family life in Kelso after the war

After demobilisation from the army, my grandfather returned to Kelso and took up his pre-war trade as a saddler and harness maker. Charlie and Winnie married on the 21st March 1921, in Kelso. It must have been a time of mixed emotions as Charlie's father (Robert Robeson) had died only eleven days before, on the 10th March. He is buried in Lilliesleaf cemetery.

Charlie and Winnie's marriage certificate

Charlie and Winnie settled down to family life in Kelso and moved into a house at 24 Horse Market in the town.

Wedding day telegraph from close friend and soldier Alf Knott, sent from his home at Bromley in Kent.

Charlie and Winnie married in 1921

Charlie at the time of his marriage to Winnie.

Winnie in her marriage year.

Winnie with Charlie's best man, Mr George Rutherford. Taken in the garden at Eden Bank House, Stichill, Kelso.

My grandparents took up their pre-war interests in the town including; rugby, golf, cricket, walking, dancing, poetry and reading

PROGRAMME

Private Subscription Dance.

✕ ✕ ✕

Town Hall, Kelso,
19th Dec., 1921.

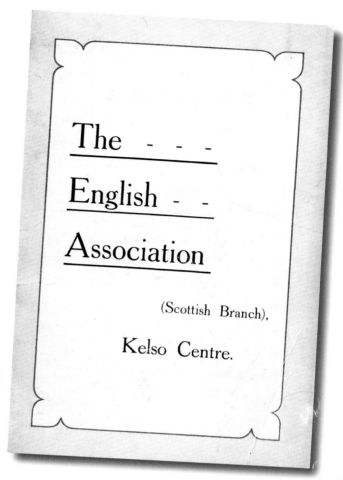

The - - -

English - -

Association

(Scottish Branch),

Kelso Centre.

Kelso

Cricket Club.

Season 1920.

Bowden Golf Club.

CONSTITUTION AND RULES

AND

RULES FOR THE GAME.

J. SMITH, PRINTER, KELSO.

Kelso from the air. How Kelso looked from the air in the 1930's (RCAHMS photo taken in 1933)

Charlie was glad to be home and renewed his interest in town life and country sports. He worked on setting up his own saddlery business.

Charlie relaxing by the banks of the Eden Water, where he loved to walk and fish.

Winnie (right) with Mrs Rutherford.

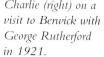

Charlie (right) on a visit to Berwick with George Rutherford in 1921.

Settling down to business and family life in Kelso in the 1920's

In 1922 Charlie purchased the saddlery business of G. Kerr and rented a property at 16 Roxburgh Street, Kelso. The sum paid for the business was £226, a significant sum of money in those days.

Charlie at his saddlery shop doorway at 16 Roxburgh Street, Kelso c.1922.

Charlie's business was located in Roxburgh Street, the 3rd shop front on the left hand side of the street.

Business life in the Borders between the wars

The Tweed, *near Peebles.*

Clydesdales - The horse power for hundreds of years was ending

(Authors collection)

Throughout the 1920's, cars, lorries and vans were slowly replacing horse- drawn traps and carriages. On farms, the first tractors were beginning to appear which reduced the dependency on man power and horse power. The number of farm labourers required to work the land fell and people moved into town for employment. By the 1930's, heavy horses such as Clydesdales and Shire horses and the demand for the leatherwork needed to halter, harness and saddle them began to decline. Leatherwork for horses was Charlie's stock-in-trade.

TOWN HALL AND SQUARE, KELSO

Throughout the 1930's the use of horses declined and motor cars became more popular.

(Authors collection)

Family life

In 1924, Charlie and Winnie's first child Robert (Robin) was born, followed by Margaret (1927), James (1930) and Mabel (1931).

Charlie and Winnie on the ferry across the Tweed to Sprouston in 1925 with son Robin (centre), accompanied by her sister Ena & her son, on left.

Charlie (right) with son Robin, who was one year old in 1925. Dougie McInnes (left) was Charlie's nephew, his sister Anne's son.

Charlie's children – A growing family to feed

Margaret and Robin - 1927.

Mabel and James in Shedden Park, Kelso - 1933.

Taken at the bandstand in Shedden Park - 1930. Margaret, Robin, James and Winnie.

As the war ended, Philip Gibbs had time to reflect on what he had witnessed and wrote…

'The world will not accept a message of despair; and millions of men to-day who went through the agony of the war are inspired by the humble belief that humanity may be cured of its cruelty and stupidity and a brotherhood of peoples more powerful than a League of Nations may be founded in the world after its present sickness and out of the conflict of its anarchy. That is the new vision which leads men on, and if we can take one step that way it will be better than the backward fall which civilisation took when Germany played the Devil and led us all into the jungle. The Devil in Germany had to be killed. There was no other way than by helping the Germans to kill it before it mastered them. Now let us master our own devils and get back to kindness towards all men of good-will. That also is the only way, to heal the heart of the world and our own state. Let us seek the beauty in life and somehow, remembering the boys that died too soon and all the falsity and hatred of these last 5 years. By blood and passion there will be no healing, for we have seen too much blood, but we must wipe it out of our souls. ….Let us have peace!'

Phillip Gibbs, War Correspondent, 1919

Great War casualty figures

The figures speak for themselves ………..worldwide, 6 million dead, 2 million wounded and 3 million missing presumed dead.

After 4 years of trench warfare, many men returned home broken men……broken in spirit and broken in mind and body. Few would lead a normal life again.

No one that was there, could ever forget the sights, the sounds, the stench of the battlefields and after all this, one over arching question remained……………………………………………………………………..........Why?

Lest We Forget

The war was won. The allies had prevailed. It was time to reflect, take stock and remember those who had given their lives. The sacrifices made by a whole generation were to be felt for many years to come.

(Authors collection)

The Fallen

"WE WILL REMEMBER THEM"

They
shall grow not old,
As we that are left grow old;
Age shall not weary them,
Nor the years condemn.
At the going down of the sun,
And in the morning
We will
Remember them.

*Laurence Binyon,
from For the Fallen.*

These lines were written by Robert Laurence Binyon in 1915, after the retreat from the battle of Mons and the victory at the battle of the Marne.

(Authors collection)

In Flanders Fields

*In Flanders fields the poppies blow
Between the crosses, row on row
That mark our place; and in the sky
The larks, still bravely singing, fly
Scare heard amid the guns below
We are the Dead. Short days ago
We lived, felt dawn, saw sunset glow,
Loved and were loved, and now we lie,
In Flanders fields.
Take up our quarrel with the foe:
To you from failing hands we throw
The torch; be yours to hold it high
If ye break faith with us who die
We shall not sleep, though poppies grow
In Flanders fields.*

By John McCrae (1915)

It was at Essex Farm, on the Western Front in Belgium, that Lt. Col. John McCrae, a Canadian Medical Officer, wrote 'In Flanders Fields'. He worked to save the lives of soldiers during the Second Battle of Ypres, in 1915. In a Field Dressing Station, he wrote the poem on a page torn from his dispatch book, between the arrival of wounded men. Having saved so many soldiers lives, John McCrae himself died of pneumonia in France in 1918.

We should never forget the debt we owe.

. REMEMBER .

(Authors collection)

Unveiling of Kelso War Memorial

Kelso War Memorial unveiling on September 25th 1921. (Alastair Brooks)

Over 4,000 people watched the ceremony. Officiating at the memorial, from left to right are: Rev D. G. Hamilton of Kelso Parish Church, Lt. General Sir J. M. Babington of Pinnaclehill House, Rev T. C. Kirkwood of Kelso United Free Church and the Duke of Roxburghe (extreme right). The memorial was designed by Robert Lorimer who was the architect for several war memorials including the National War Memorial at Edinburgh Castle.

The bronze panels beneath the Union Flags record the names of 243 men of Kelso and District who fell in the Great War.

My grandparents, were at the ceremony to pay their respects, to give thanks to those friends that lived and to remember those that died.

"God gave all men all earth to love,
But since our hearts are small,
Ordained for each one spot should prove,
Beloved over all."

Rudyard Kipling

For Charlie & Winnie & Kelso & Home!

The Town of Kelso and River Tweed

(Authors collection)

'Sweet is the memory of a distant friend,
Like the mellow rays of a departing sun,
They fall tenderly, though sadly on the heart.'

By Washington Irving and written by
Charlie, in Winnie's autograph book, in 1916.

Words which reflect
the thoughts of a
generation.

(Authors collection)

Charles Robeson was extremely fortunate to survive three years on the Frontline during the Great War. Winnie was there at home, in support, all the way through. Many of their close friends were not so lucky. Both my grandparents left a poignant historical and social record that will hopefully, be of interest to future generations of Scottish Borderers.

'Small service is true service, while it lasts,
Of friends however humble-scorn not one,
The daisy by the shadow that it casts,
Protects the lingering dew drop from the sun.'

By William Wordsworth and written by
Charlie, in Winnie's autograph book in 1916.

Winnie Robeson

Charlie Robeson

They were children of the late Victorian & Edwardian era and theirs was a remarkable, self reliant and community spirited generation.

Select Bibliography

This book is a compilation of information gleaned from several web sites, books, photographic collections, family postcards and family letters. As a consequence, the historical information contained in this book, is largely a bringing together and distillation of existing written and pictorial information and is largely credited as such, within the text. I take no credit for any of it and I acknowledge this in full. I take responsibility however, for any errors which may be present. All information is given in good faith.

I would like to acknowledge the following main sources of information, with gratitude:

Websites:

The Long Long Trail by Chris Baker – www.1914-1918.net

BBC History – www.bbc.co.uk/history

Books:

History of Kelso Rugby Football Club: The first 100 years – Arthur Hastie

Complete History of Oldham RLFC – Michael Turner

The Somme & Passchendaele – Chris McCarthy

Realities of War & From Bapaume to Passchendaele – Philip Gibbs

Letters from the Trenches – Bill Lamin

For King and Country and the Scottish Borderers – Gavin Richardson

Chronicles of the Great War – Peter Simkins

The Great War Explained – Philip Stevens

War Record of the 4th Battalion KOSB and Lothian and Border Horse, 1920

Other Sources:

Tom Tulloch Marshall – Independent Military Researcher

War Diaries: National Archives, London

Official War Photographs: National Library of Scotland (NLS), Edinburgh & Imperial War Museum (IWM), London

Robeson Family photographs

Personal Acknowledgements & Thanks

This work could not have been completed without the assistance and encouragement from the following people (and organisations), whom I thank:

Foremost my family; Ghislaine, Jamie, Lucy-Jane and Josie Robeson

Special thanks to Alastair Campbell for encouragement during our compiling of 'Kelso Memories' and Alastair's (sadly unfulfilled) hope to see 'Son of Kelso on the Somme' published

Keith Robeson, Douglas Robeson, Mairi Robeson, Margaret Carlaw, Chris Badenoch, Hector Innes, Clive Dibbern, Maggie McGee, Alastair Brooks, Ruth Holmes, Margot Laurie & Dave Welsh

Simon Gaunt, book designer, Footeprint, Jedburgh

Margaret Jeary for proof reading

Alison Metcalf, Manuscripts Curator, National Library of Scotland, Edinburgh

Judy Noakes, Copyright Advisor, National Archives, London

Charlie Robertson, Rector (retired) Kelso High School

Edwardian & WW1 postcard manufacturers

Scottish Borders Council

National Library of Scotland

Imperial War Museum

Scotland's Rural College

The various sales points

The Fallago Fund

Tweed Forum

RCAHMS